Sustainable
Homes

SUSTAINABLE HOMES

James Grayson Trulove
with Nora Richter Greer
foreword by Dennis Wedlick

COLLINS DESIGN
An Imprint of HarperCollinsPublishers

SUSTAINABLE HOMES: 26 Designs that Respect the Earth
Copyright © 2004 by COLLINS DESIGN and James Grayson Trulove

HarperCollins books may be purchased for educational, business, or sales promotional use. For information, please write: Special Markets Department, HarperCollins Publishers Inc., 10 East 53rd Street, New York, NY 10022.

First published in 2001 as *Hot Dirt Cool Straw* by:
HBI, *An Imprint of* HarperCollins*Publishers*

Now Published by:
Collins Design
An Imprint of HarperCollins*Publishers*
10 East 53rd Street
New York, NY 10022
Tel: (212) 207-7000
Fax: (212) 207-7654
collinsdesign@harpercollins.com
www.harpercollins.com

Distributed throughout the world by:
HarperCollins*Publishers*
10 East 53rd Street
New York, NY 10022-5299
Fax: (212) 207-7654

Packaged by:
Grayson Publishing
1250 28th Street NW
Washington, D.C. 20007
Tel: (202) 337-1380
Fax: (202) 337-1381

Library of Congress Control Number: 2005938369

ISBN-10: 0-06-059446-2
ISBN-13: 978-0-06-059446-6

Printed in Hong Kong
Second Printing, 2006

1 2 3 4 5 6 7 8 9 /05 04 03

While concern for environmental issues and sustainability are increasingly a part of discussions between clients and their architects, these concerns are integral to the houses presented in *Sustainable Homes*. And equally important, these houses combine environmental sensitivity with uncommonly creative solutions to the many design-related problems associated with sustainability. With a few exceptions, most of these houses are, at first glance, distinguished not by the materials with which they are constructed, nor by their integration into the landscape, nor by the often heroic efforts undertaken to make them more energy efficient. Rather, it is the house's design that first attracts attention. It is only after careful study that the close connection between the two reveals itself.

To better understand the contributions that each house makes in *Sustainable Homes*, a simple system of color-coding has been employed to highlight the dominant sustainable features of each structure. This coding appears on the contents page opposite and in conjunction with each house featured.

The key to the coding is as follows:

■ Blue indicates special consideration was given to the way in which the house was integrated into the landscape.

■ Green indicates a dominant use of sustainable/replenishable building materials.

■ Red indicates exceptional measures undertaken to insure energy efficiency.

Contents

Foreword by Dennis Wedlick   7

Kutcher Residence   Brian MacKay-Lyons Architecture   10

Hester/McNally Residence   Arkin-Tilt Architects   18

Arroyo House   Line and Space/Les Wallach   24

Sonoma Coast House   Obie G. Bowman, Architect   30

Summer House   C.V. Hølmebakk   38

West Marin House   Fernau & Hartman   44

MacKenzie House   Travis Price Architects   56

Gordon House   Gordon & Gordon Architects   62

Alves Residence   Harahan + Meyers Architects   70

Johnson/Jones Residence   Jones Studio, Inc.   80

Oregon Coast House   Obie G. Bowman, Architect   88

Palmer/Rose House   Rick Joy Architect   96

Mackie House   Dan Rockhill and Associates   110

Danielson Cottage   Brian MacKay-Lyons Architecture   116

Tennis House   Gray Organschi Architecture   122

Lakeside Residence   Overland Partners   130

Howard House   Brian MacKay-Lyons Architecture   138

Low Compound   Jones Studio, Inc.   146

Pins Sur Mer   Obie G. Bowman, Architect   154

Villa Eila   Heikkinen-Komonen Architects   162

Mouney House   DeBoer Architects   168

Hansen Residence   Line and Space   174

South Texas Ranch House   Lake/Flato Architects   180

Tin Roof House   Obie G. Bowman Architect   188

McDevitt House   Studio A Architecture   194

Yost House   Studio A Architecture   202

FOREWORD

BY DENNIS WEDLICK

For generations, becoming a homeowner has been a landmark event for many Americans. Although some seventy percent of us live in urban or suburban areas with more than enough existing housing, most of us aspire to live in a newly built house. This desire does more than reflect our nation's culture; it is also a barometer of our nation's optimism. One of our most-watched economic indicators is the construction of new homes. When people have the confidence to purchase or build a new home, they generally have confidence in their future.

With an ever-expanding population, the question is whether or not the desire to own a newly built home is sustainable. At some point in the near future will environmental damage force people to abandon this goal? Will the cost of supplies and utilities drive the price of building a new home so high that it would be completely out of reach for all but a few? Will the negative impacts of mining and deforestation eventually outweigh the economic benefits of new housing developments? Will fewer permeable surfaces overburden our drainage and sewage infrastructure? Will regional water and energy supplies not be able to meet the demands of more newer, larger homes?

All of these questions address real problems that home builders and government agencies face today in regions across the country. This is not to mention the seemingly insurmountable problems of indoor air pollution, global warming, and biodiversity depletion. When the majority of the nation cannot possibly afford to own new homes, or are severely restricted in building them, new home construction will essentially stop. After all, a new home is not an absolute need. Shelter can be had in many ways. Should this come to pass the dream of building a new home will vanish.

This would be a tragedy for the creativity and culture of our nation, not just for the economy. There is no greater potential for personal expression than building one's own shelter. For this reason alone, every effort should be made to enable new home construction to be sustainable for generations to come. Over the last four decades, designers and builders have experimented, and succeeded, in producing excellent examples of new methods of construction that could be classified as environmentally friendly. Today, we realize that to be truly sustainable, it is not enough to imagine methods of minimizing damage to the environment; instead the results must have a net positive impact on it. In other words, the construction of a new house needs to provide a net improvement for the environment, to offer more than if no construction took place.

At first this would seem impossible. How could encouraging construction be better for the environment than limiting it? Imagine:

- A new house built in a desert that not only treads lightly on the landscape but also generates more energy than it consumes.
- A house built on an arid mountainside that collects and purifies more water than its owners use.
- A row of town houses in an overcrowded city that provides more green space than previously available.
- A construction industry using materials recycled from the waste of other industries that would otherwise pollute our waterways or require more landfills.
- Offshoot industries producing interior furnishings, fabrics, and finishes that find profits in providing cleaner, healthier products.
- Residential design that not only satisfies the desires for personal expression but also raises awareness about our fragile environment.

PREVIOUS PAGE, LEFT: Sonoma Coast House, Obie Bowman Architect; photography: Tom Rider. OPPOSITE: House in West Marin, Fernau and Hartman Architects; photography: Todd Hido.

All of these opportunities exist today, and *Sustainable Homes* provides example after example of the possibilities for net positive results in residential construction when the designers and the home owners choose sustainable design.

There is no simple list of elements that must be included in the design of a sustainable home. Every design must be appropriate for the home owner's needs, property, budget, and aesthetic goals. There are however, criteria by which we can judge the success of a new home's potential for sustainability:

• The design should consider the resources required for the construction or operation of the home. Sustainable homes built of straw bale; homes that incorporate salvage materials; and homes that are super insulated are all good examples of meeting these criteria. As are design specifications that call for resources for construction that are renewable or are reclaimed materials. A highly energy efficient structure or one that generates energy is an excellent model of a sustainable home that takes into account our limited resources.

• The design should promote manufacturing, construction methods, or systems that are better for the environment. Sustainable homes that are built from products that are manufactured free of toxic chemicals are not only healthier for the occupants, but also promote industries whose products are healthier for their employees. Homes that minimize waste during construction are not only more cost effective, but also easier on our environment. Designing a house with a system for treating "gray water"(wastewater from sinks, tubs, washing machines, and dishwashers) is a benefit to the water supply at large. These all meet the second goal of sustainability.

• The results of the design should encourage more sustainable design. Sustainable homes meet the third criterion by promoting other sustainable designs through different means. These homes may raise awareness of our tenuous relationship with the environment, or they may serve as an educational instrument by example. The homes' designs may highlight the surrounding natural landscape, thereby encouraging their preservation, or the excellence of the designs themselves may provide inspiration for others to consider building sustainable homes.

• In any event, the design should consider the future of the home. Sustainable homes satisfy the fourth criterion by being constructed in such a way as to easily permit reuse of the building for other purposes. Another option would be for the home's construction components to be easily disassembled and reused in future construction. A more permanent sustainable design is one that skillfully blends into context of its surroundings further insuring its preservation.

The bottom line for me as an architect is that sustainable design not be an egocentric exercise. Sustainable design is not centric in any fashion. It should mimic nature, where each action facilitates life's cycle. The seed of a tree lies in its fruit, which is the food for the animal that may find shelter under the tree. The animal's waste not only helps spread the seeds but also may fertilize the earth to encourage their growth. Every design of nature involves the entire environment and in some way sustains it. Every individual new home should follow this example and consider the larger environment and help sustain it. Early twentieth-century architects proposed that new homes should be "machines for living." Then, the revolution was to invent a residential architecture that facilitated the lives of the occupants. Now, we need new homes that are machines for a better environment.

Sustainable design is a creative and fulfilling enterprise offering the designer and home-owner new opportunities for both personal expression and personal growth. From antiquity, residential design has always been inspired by nature. Today, we have the power to restore nature through sustainable design. The houses that follow provide ample evidence that good design and sustainable design can be equal partners.

Dennis Wedlick is a nationally recognized architect who designed the 1995 Life *magazine Dream House. He is also the author of* The Good Home *(2001) and* Designing the Good Home *(2003). Wedlick is currently teaching sustainable design studios at the University of Pennsylvania and the Parsons School of Design. He lives and practices in New York City.*

KUTCHER RESIDENCE

Herring Cove, Nova Scotia, Canada

Brian MacKay-Lyons

Architecture Urban Design

Photography: James Steeves

ABOVE: The Kutcher house perches on a giant granite building outcrop high above the shipping lanes.
RIGHT: The house becomes a welcoming beacon at night.

Architect Brian MacKay-Lyons conceived of the living pavilion of the Kutcher Residence as a serene sanctuary overlooking the shipping lanes. The natural surrounding is reason enough to feel elevated. MacKay-Lyons heightened that anticipation by manipulating the entrance to the house. And, too, for the design of this house, perched on a giant granite boulder outcrop, MacKay-Lyons relies on his understanding of the local building culture—what materials will stand up to the rigors of the Nova Scotia climate, yet he uses those materials in a highly unique manner.

The visitor first passes through a gap in a 112-foot-long concrete wall at a 12-foot by 21-foot angled iron gate and then passes through the entry courtyard. Flanked by the house, shed, gate, and rock face, the pathway corkscrews up through the steel scissors stair, finally arriving at the living pavilion. This progression brings a true understanding of pavilion's structure, an elevated platform, a four-bay great room, punctuated by five pairs of steel "I" columns. It is protected at the back (the north end) by the service zone and bracketed at the east and west ends by a pair of identical hearths. The outlook is framed by a wraparound floor-to-ceiling, 100-foot glass wall, which is constantly animated by passing supertankers, fishing boats, and container ships.

The building is grounded by the long, poured concrete wall, which is then reinforced by the concrete court slab, stair treads, raised health plinths, and great room gutter. Structural steel columns allow the building to float above the rock and are reinforced by steel stairs, railings, and gate. Plywood shear fins transfer horizontal wind loads into the concrete hunches. The standing seam Galvalume wrapper folds and extrudes to protect the interior.

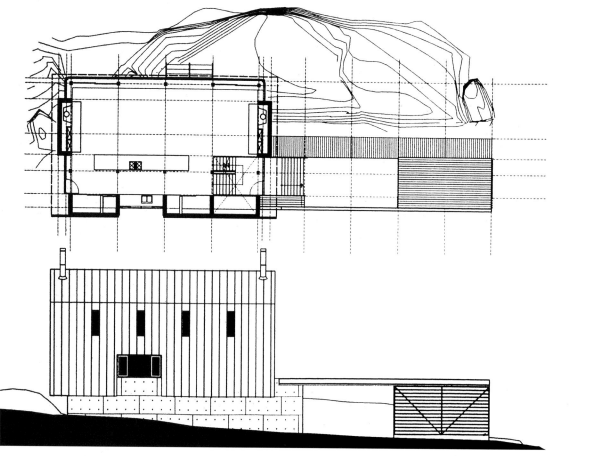

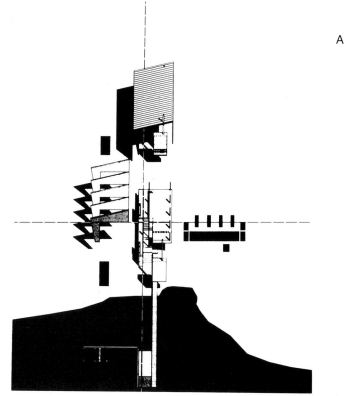

12 Kutcher Residence

TOP, MIDDLE, LEFT: Various views of the façade treatment.

ABOVE: *The standing seam roof folds over the top of the house and meets the first floor glass wall.*
LEFT: *The concrete wall and entrance gate.*

15

ABOVE: The kitchen is set at the rear of the house, opposite the front window.
RIGHT: There are two hearths—one at the east end and one at the west end of the main living space.
LEFT: Two views from the living room out through the first floor glass wall.

HESTER/MCNALLY RESIDENCE

Berkeley, California
Arkin-Tilt Architects

Photography: Ed Caldwell

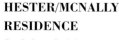

ABOVE: *Made with recycled lumber,*
the kitchen window overlooks the
garden and frog pond.
RIGHT: *The curved-roof addition is*
sheathed in license plate shingles,
the plates having been collected by
the home owners.

By incorporating "found" objects and recycled materials into its design and connecting the interior to the small garden, this remodeling brought a new exuberance for its owners—two authors and professors of ecology and community design, while demonstrating sustainability as a primary goal.

The house in question is a typical four-room, 1920s Berkeley bungalow, which had a cramped, north-facing eat-in kitchen that had little connection to the garden. The garden has been nurtured by the owners for fifteen years and contains a wide collection of found objects, plants, a pond, chickens, and ducks. The remodeling had three goals: expand the kitchen to the east without impinging on the garden or the circulation path; relocate the laundry from the existing shed; and replace the defunct fireplace and provide new transom windows from the kitchen to the living room.

To accomplish this, Arkin-Tilt Architects added a 28-square-foot addition to the 700-square-foot-house. It takes the form of a curved roof and counterpoints the bungalow in both form and materials, arching up over the existing shed to bring high southern light into the kitchen. It is sheathed in license plate "shingles" (from the owners' collection). A simple deck of reclaimed redwood mediates between inside and out and large windows and a glazed door provide ample visual connection to the garden.

To make the kitchen feel larger, the laundry shed was transformed into an intimate sitting area, which has been dubbed the "frog viewing area," as it overlooks a sunken bathtub that serves as a frog pond. The salvaged window is set low to focus the view on the lush garden while shielding the house next door. Modifications to the paneled living room were minimal.

EXISTING FLOOR PLAN

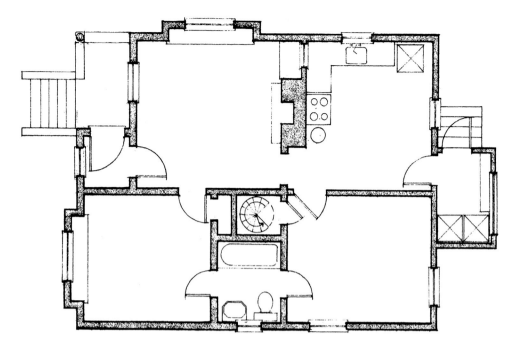

NEW FLOOR PLAN

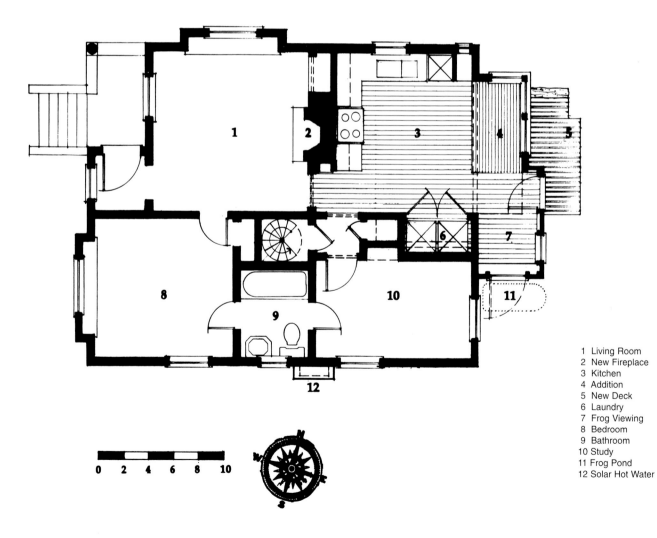

1 Living Room
2 New Fireplace
3 Kitchen
4 Addition
5 New Deck
6 Laundry
7 Frog Viewing
8 Bedroom
9 Bathroom
10 Study
11 Frog Pond
12 Solar Hot Water

0 2 4 6 8 10

20 Hester/McNally Residence

SITE/ROOF PLAN

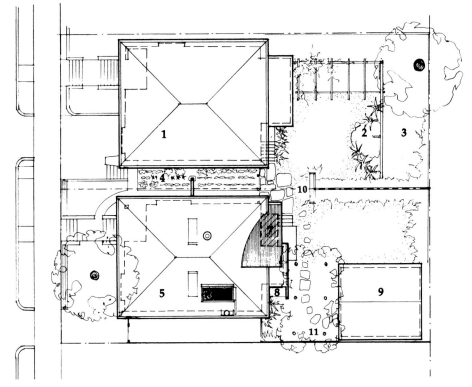

1 Office
2 Duck Pond
3 Chicken Yard
4 Vegetables
5 Residence
6 Solar Panel
7 Addition
8 Frog Pond
9 Studio
10 Rock Collection
11 Hub Cap Art

AXONOMETRIC VIEW

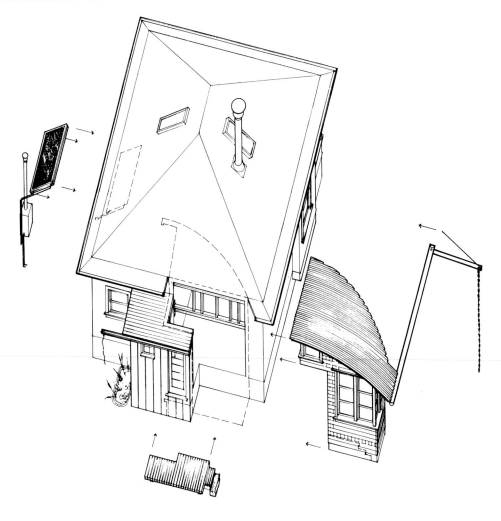

ABOVE: The remodeling brought light and space to the once-cramped kitchen. The cabinetry was kept simple to highlight the terrazzo-like recycled glass counter tops.
RIGHT: Trimmed to match the paneling, transoms allow daylight to penetrate the interiors.

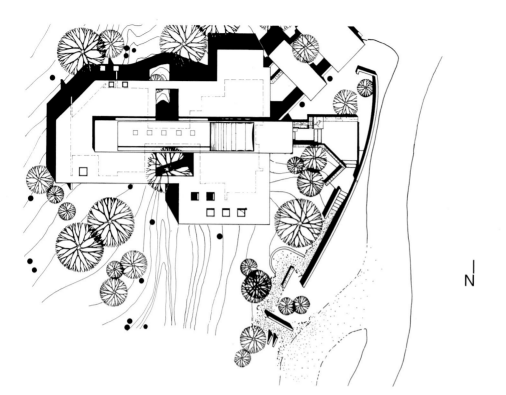

ARROYO HOUSE

Tucson, Arizona

Line and Space/Les Wallach

Located in the Sonoran desert near Tucson, the Arroyo House sits gently on its desert site, as if a mirage—a long, low, iridescent building that traverses a natural gully as it embraces its desert surrounding.

To cause minimal disturbance to the sensitive ecosystem, Line and Space separated the 3,000-square-foot house into public and private realms on two sides of a delicate arroyo, connecting the sections by a covered bridge. Elsewhere, cantilevered concrete decks gently meet the edge of the natural wash and original rocks. To further integrate the house to its site, salvaged stone from a nearby highway project complement the walls of gray, split-faced concrete block.

The roof's area equals 8,000 square feet, well over twice the floor area. Large overhangs keep out the scorching summer sun, yet allow the lower-angled winter sun to warm the house. This configuration, along with the use of double-glazed low "E" windows, allow floor-to-ceiling glazed walls on the north and south elevations to take advantage of the magnificent views, and in effect, dematerialize the boundaries between inside and out. Skylights that invite warming daylight in winter are equipped with a retractable canvas cloth to keep out the severe rays in the summer.

Concerned with spatial sensory transitions, the architect thoughtfully designed entry sequences to avoid visual shocks as the visitor moves from the bright glare of the sun to the shade of the covered entry to the lower light levels of interior spaces. In addition, abrupt temperature changes are avoided by gradually bringing the visitor in from the intense heat to the shaded entry via evaporatively cooled decks and finally to the air-conditioned interior.

Photography: Colby Campbell, Glen Christiansen, Mark Feirer

RIGHT: The house sits lean and low on its desert site.

FLOOR PLAN

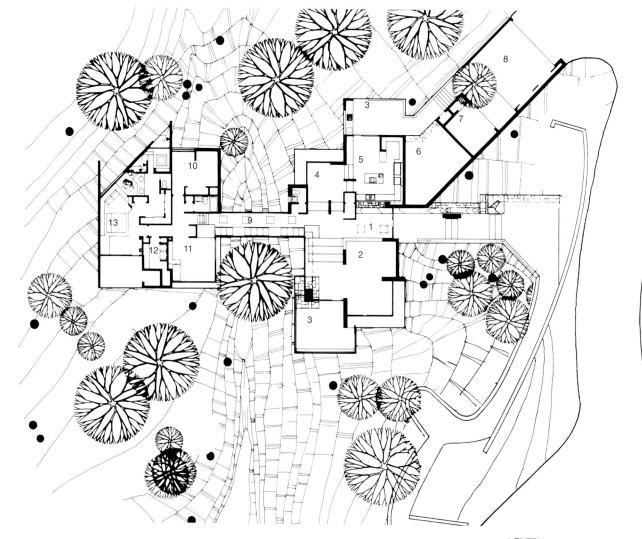

1 ENTRY
2 LIVING ROOM
3 EXTERIOR DECK
4 DINING ROOM
5 KITCHEN
6 SAND PLAY YARD
7 SHOP·
8 GARAGE
9 BRIDGEWAY
10 BEDROOM
11 LIBRARY/STUDY
12 LAUNDRY
13 MASTER BEDROOM

SECTION

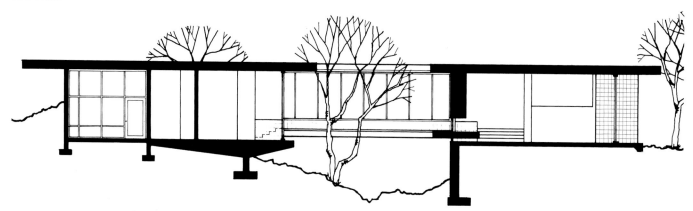

26 Arroyo House

ABOVE: Two sculptural "sentinels"
painted blue to match the sky greet
visitors to the residence.
ABOVE RIGHT: The stone veneer
entrance wall.
RIGHT: Steps lead up along the stone
veneer entrance wall.

ABOVE: *View into the living room.*
LEFT: *The bridge that crosses the arroyo and connects the public and private realms of the house.*
RIGHT: *Construction of cantilevered decks conserved much of the natural environment.*

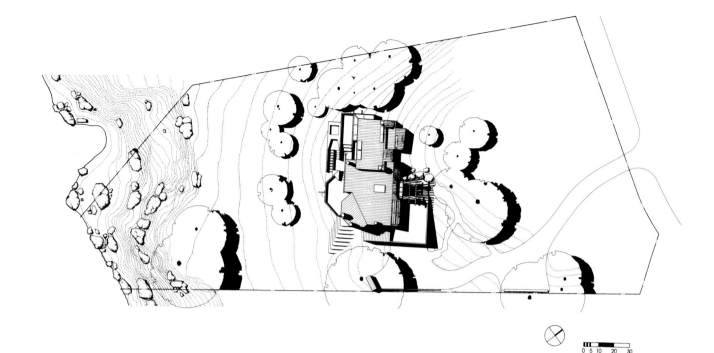

0 5 10   20   30

SONOMA COAST HOUSE

Sonoma County, California
Obie G. Bowman Architect

Photography: Tom Rider

An unusual transformation has come to Sonoma Coast House thirty years after the house was first built. Redesigned by Obie Bowman, the once dark and isolated house now seems to have existed among the pine trees forever, only its ventilation chimneys acknowledging the activities transpiring within.

The additions to the house were intended to connect the interior with the surrounding trees, and allow the house to "snuggle among the vegetation with its four ventilation chimneys pointing skyward." Only 850 square feet were added to the footprint of the existing house, yet the interior was completely reworked functionally and structurally. A new level was added beneath the first floor. The existing battered walls were retained, added onto, and sheathed with standing seam copper. The chimneys are used to bleed off summer heat build-up from the extensive southwesterly glazing, which can be a real concern with a vacation house that is unoccupied for many weeks at a time.

Visitors approach the house from the easterly side by a meandering stone path that passes beneath an old, magnificent Monterey pine and ends at a massive trellis designed to support giant honeysuckle. Set between the kitchen and dining rooms, the entry descends to a split-function living room. To the right is a fireplace and television placed within walls of exposed framing with treated-cooper backing. To the left is a glazed octagonal tower with timber-frame construction that uses debarked Douglas fir log columns.

Bowman uses the octagonal tower as a significant design element. It brings daylight deep into the house, connects the interior with the structure of the large Monterey cypress pine, and offers views from the upper dining and kitchen area as well as the library and living rooms.

RIGHT: The intent of the redesign was to snuggle the house among the pine trees. The site is viewed here from the coastal bluff.

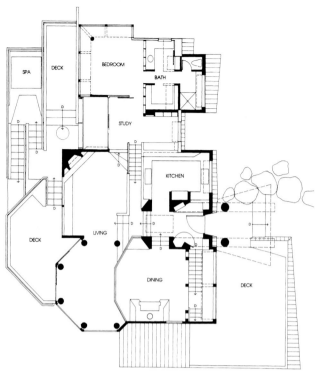

○⊘ UPPER LEVEL FLOOR PLAN

0   5   10

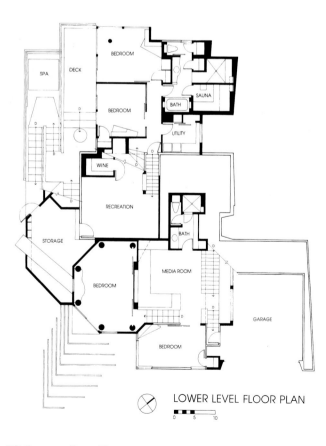

○⊘ LOWER LEVEL FLOOR PLAN

0   5   10

RIGHT: Southeast façade viewed from the bluff.
LEFT: The fireplace, with treated copper backing, was placed within walls of exposed framing.
LEFT BELOW: View from dining room through braced frame and sloped glazing to old Monterey pine.

CROSS SECTION

0   5   10

CLOCKWISE FROM TOP LEFT: *Stairs to the study with the kitchen at right; entry with the kitchen at left; and view from the living room towards the study, kitchen, and dining room.* LEFT: *View from dining room to living room and study beyond.* FOLLOWING PAGES: *Northeast façade showing entry trellis.*

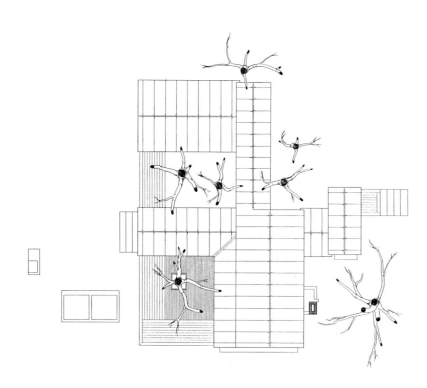

SUMMER HOUSE

Risør, Norway
C.V. Hølmebakk Architect

Photography: C.V. Hølmebakk,
P. Bernsten

RIGHT: *The house was designed to precisely fit among the small grove of pine trees.*

The story behind the design of this house reads like a fairy tale, yet any dreamlike qualities give way quickly to an exact precision. After spending twenty-five years at their summer house on the south coast of Norway, a couple decided to give the house to their children and grandchildren and build another elsewhere on the site. Their first choice was to build among a grove of seven old pine trees, on a sloping stone-covered area with a marvelous view to the sea.

Architect Carl-Viggo Hølmebakk's solution was a foundation of "adjustable" concrete pillars. The dimensions of the main wooden beams were calculated so that the pillars could be moved in one direction or another if they interfered with the tree's root system. More than thirty pillars were erected on the site; no roots were cut.

The house design was carefully planned in accordance with the trunks and branches of the old trees. The complete column and beam system was precut and profiled in laminated wood. The structural skeleton was joined by steel mountings. Walls, windows, and doors were installed in the skeleton, leaving the columns exposed on both sides. The tuning of spatial qualities and views—the apportion of closed walls, glass panels and windows—were verified at the site and some were decided during the building process.

While the house is relatively small, the experience of the interior is extended through the use of outdoor porches, stairs, and open courts. In fact, during the day, the "living room" extends to the wooden terrace and the naked rock floor on the west side of the house. The space is furnished with facilities for outdoor cooking and an herb garden.

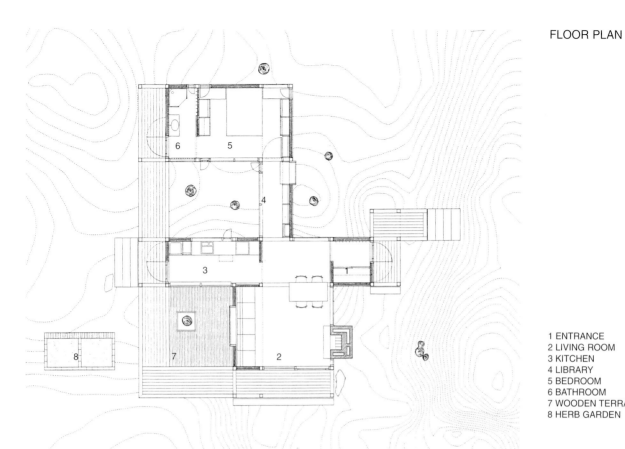

1 ENTRANCE
2 LIVING ROOM
3 KITCHEN
4 LIBRARY
5 BEDROOM
6 BATHROOM
7 WOODEN TERRACE
8 HERB GARDEN

SECTIONS

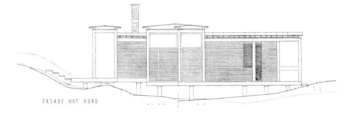

FASADE MOT NORD

FASADE MOT ØST

FASADE MOT SYD

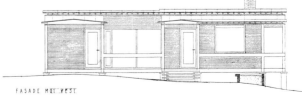

FASADE MOT VEST

40 Summer House

RIGHT, TOP: *The entrance stairs are set on large boulders.*
RIGHT, MIDDLE: *The view from the bedroom out over the courtyard towards the kitchen.*
RIGHT: *View over the court looking toward the library.*
LEFT: *A pine tree hugs one side of the master bedroom.*

ABOVE: The house was successfully built around the trees through the use of "adjustable" concrete pillars. RIGHT: The library window.

42 Summer House

ABOVE: *The small size of the house was visually and physically extended by the outdoor patios, courts, and stairs.*

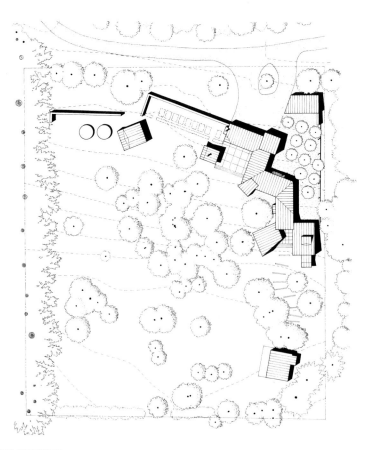

WEST MARIN HOUSE

Marin County, California
Fernau & Hartman
Architects, Inc.

Photography: Todd Hido

The mild climate in Northern California supports an indoor-outdoor style of living centered around the courtyard. For the West Marin House, Richard Fernau and Laura Hartman designed a highly energy efficient model that unfolds in a richly experimental and episodic manner.

The house is sited on the upper corner of a gently sloped, large wooded lot above Bolinas Lagoon. Here, Fernau and Hartman set a one-room house that zigzags across the property. It's basically an "L"-shaped courtyard plan, but broken up into a series of three courtyards. The house itself is broken into three fundamental activity zones—for eating, playing, and resting. Sewn into this basic framework are "pockets" for work, friends, and reflection. And, in turn, each zone has its own courtyard. In other words, each activity has an "interior and exterior manifestation."

The clients were interested in building with straw bale, but were also looking for a contemporary, site-specific design. This inspired a final design in which straw bale walls alternate with thinner, glass-dominated walls, allowing the house to open up to the view of the garden and mountains in the distance.

The design is actually a modification of a prototype developed by the architects as an "antidote for an overly compartmentalized urban existence." The goal is a "situated building" inextricable from its site, where distinctions between interior and exterior are moot. In the case of the West Marin House, the design works exceedingly well to tie the house to its site, both in near and distant views, and the forms echo the vernacular of rural northern California.

RIGHT: The modified courtyard house is situated on a gentle, wooded slope.

44 West Marin House

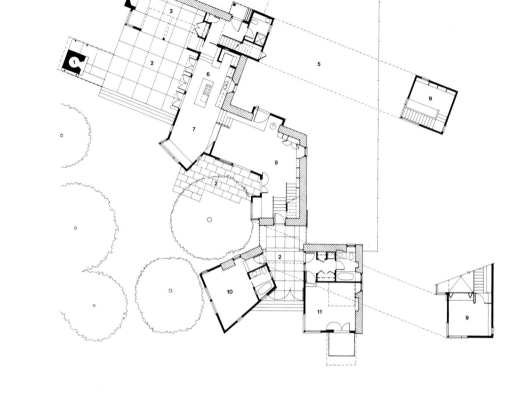

1 PIZZA OVEN
2 COURTYARD
3 LIVING ROOM/PORCH
4 BOAT HOUSE
5 ORCHARD
6 COOKING
7 EATING
8 WORK/PLAY
9 STUDY
10 KIDS' BEDROOM
11 MASTER BEDROOM

0 5 10

LEFT: A model of the house.

46 West Marin House

RIGHT, TOP AND RIGHT: The zigzag floor plan offers frequent opportunities for window fenestration.
FOLLOWING PAGES: The cooking and eating module provides ample open space for entertaining.

ABOVE, LEFT, AND RIGHT: Each module connects to the outside courtyard, as seen in the living space. Ceilings are exposed beams.

50 West Marin House

ABOVE AND RIGHT: An abundance of natural light enters the living area.

LEFT, ABOVE, AND RIGHT: The bedrooms offer privacy yet also a sense of spaciousness and light.

MACKENZIE HOUSE

Vargas Island,
Vancouver, Canada
Travis Price Architects

Photography: Kenneth M. Wyner,
Ian Mackenzie

ABOVE: *The design included the bridge along the path to the house.* RIGHT: *At night, the glazed and fiberglass walls of the house are identifiable.*

When writer/landscape photographer Ian MacKenzie decided to build his personal wilderness refuge on a 3,000-hectare island off the west coast of Vancouver Island, he wanted the forest untouched—and even the sense of the forest unaltered. He turned to architect Travis Price who built a house of steel, glass, and fiberglass and decorated it with colorful symbols similar to the long houses of the Nuu-cha-nulth (the West Coast people) and the island ancestors, the Ahoushat Indians.

MacKenzie grew up on Vancouver Island and much admires the natural environment there and its Douglas fir trees. Yet, both he and Price knew that the material would not stand up to the rigors of the Pacific Northwest climate. The house and the small guest house, therefore, are constructed of steel construction, with fiberglass sheeting, glass doors and windows, and driftwood planks (mostly cedar, which is especially hard and long-lasting) that were piled up on the beach. Both are simple forms, the main house resembling a pagoda and the guest house a tent.

Located on Clayoquot Sound, half of Vargas Island is classified as a state park and only six other houses exist there. All the materials for Mackenzie's house had to be brought to the island by boat and carried across slippery rocks to the building site. The main house stands on a small peninsula a few meters from the sea. The guest house, with its transparent walls and roof, is farther in the forest.

The main house is painted with nautical symbols—starfish, crabs, and snails. The two gable windows below the roof are shaped like a whale's tail and whale's mouth. Electricity comes through a solar panel and light from a propane gas lamp. Water is pumped by hand.

56 MacKenzie House

SIDE ELEVATION

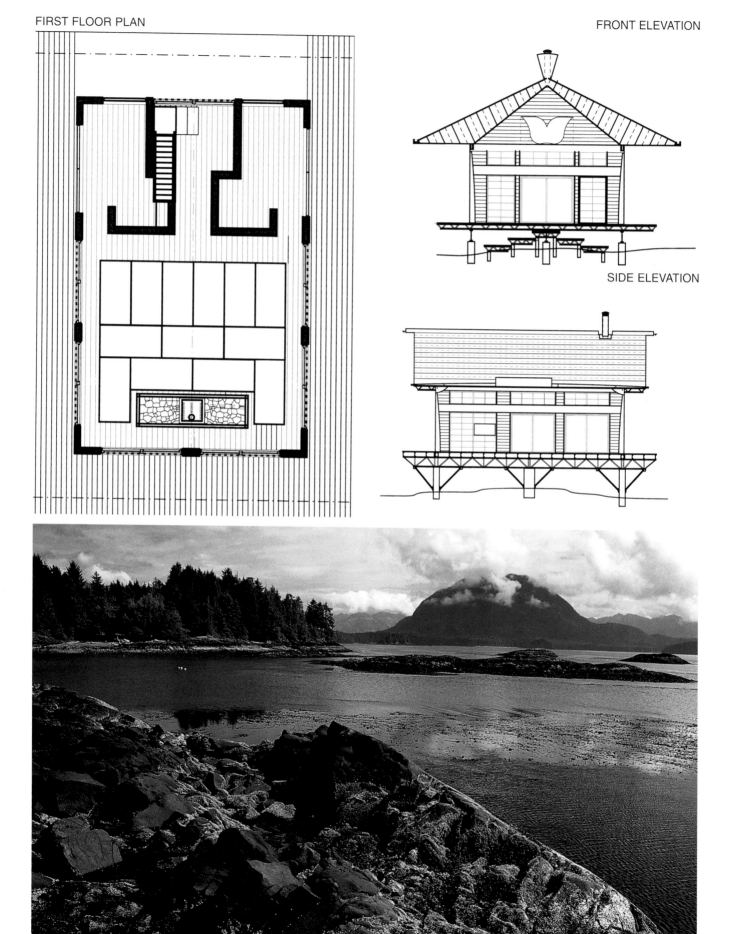

58 MacKenzie House

RIGHT, TOP: *Detail of the stainless steel "eco-gods" positioned at the building's corner.*
RIGHT, MIDDLE: *The meditation bridge overlooking Clayoquot Sound.*
RIGHT: *The guest cottage is set in the forest apart from the main house.*
LEFT: *View from the house across Clayoquot Sound.*

ABOVE AND RIGHT: The interior seen at different times, in different lights, from different angles, and in different moods.

60 MacKenzie House

GORDON HOUSE

Lakeville, Connecticut
Gordon & Gordon
Architecture & Landscape
Design

Photography: Peter Aaron/Esto

RIGHT: A blanket of juniper covers the house. Bluestone terraces edge the rear of the house.

To "preserve the natural setting and conserve resources," architect and landscape architect G. Mackenzie Gordon built his house underground. Actually, he set the ranch-style home into a sloping site so that from the south elevation it appears merely as a series of blue stone terraces blanketed by junipers.

The house is located on eight acres of former farmland in northwestern Connecticut. "This open, sloping site lent itself to building below ground," Gordon says, "which preserves the natural setting while helping to conserve resources."

As one approaches the 3,200-square-foot house down a winding lane, a detached garage helps frame an arrival court. Utilitarian, yet sculptural, forms rise from the juniper, including an abbreviated chimney, wedge-shaped clerestory structures backed with solar panels, and a spiral-stair tower that mimics a silo. The residential nature of the place is only realized from the other side—the north side, where a bank of windows captures the views out through a mountain valley into neighboring Massachusetts.

Gordon designed the interior spaces to conceal, as much as possible, the underground nature of the house. The main living and dining spaces run along the length of the windowed façade, while the bedrooms, bathrooms, mechanical room, and kitchen are stacked against the earth embankment. Skylights bring in natural light and help lessen the feeling of being underground.

Materials are simple. All foundations, columns, exterior walls, parapet, roof, and floor slabs are concrete. Interior partitions and the roof beneath the solar collectors are framed in wood. Exterior windows and door frames are rendered in maple and teak.

FLOOR PLAN

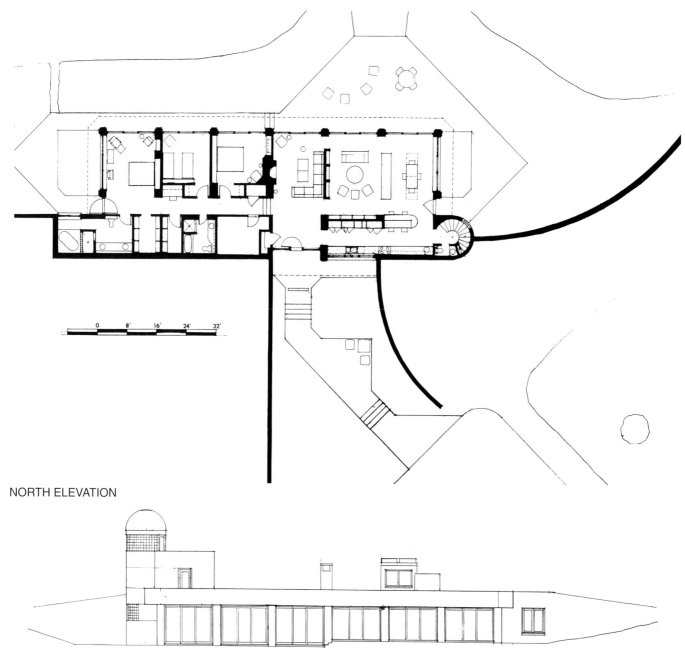

0   8'   16'   24'   32'

NORTH ELEVATION

EAST ELEVATION

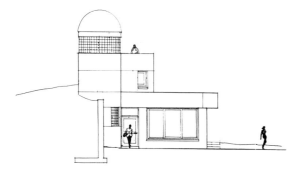

WEST ELEVATION

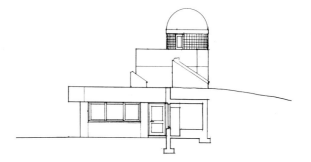

64 Gordon House

ABOVE: *Walkway leading to the rear entrance. Eventually, the concrete retaining wall will be covered with juniper.*

LEFT AND ABOVE: The spiral staircase is housed in the silo-like structure, which can be easily seen from front and back.
RIGHT, TOP: A solar-panel structure sits among the other structures on the landscaped roof.
RIGHT: Shrubbery becomes the railing atop the house.
FOLLOWING PAGES: The main living spaces are aligned along the window façade with views across the valley into Massachusetts.

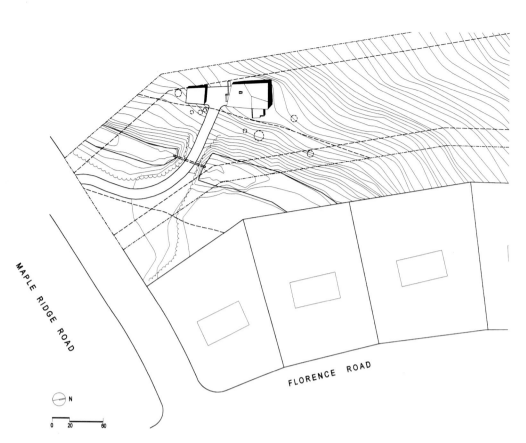

ALVES RESIDENCE

Northampton, Massachusetts
Hanrahan + Meyers
Architects

Photography: Eduard Hueber,
Rhett Russo

RIGHT: The ark-like house was
designed as a "single modulated
volume."

The client envisioned a house with the "primal quality of a single room"—almost cave-like in character—that captured within it as much daylight as possible. Architect/client discussions progressed to wooden structures built in Massachusetts by carpenters skilled in ship construction, even referencing *Moby Dick*. (In that epic novel, Herman Melville describes a small church constructed as a ship.) The result is an abstraction by architects Thomas Hanrahan and Victoria Meyers of a single vessel into a house—or, in other words, the design of a house as a single modulated volume excavated by light.

The 1,900-square-foot house sits on a triangular shelf of flat land on a steeply sloping hillside facing south and east as it falls toward an intermittent stream at its base. The structure is an elongated volume to match the site and is entered from a stone terrace cut through a deep, sculptural wall on the south end. Inside, a steel stair drops from the second floor deck containing the master bedroom. Covering this floating deck and the first floor is a "shell" made of shiplapped cedar. Extending through this shell off the master bedroom is a second floor outdoor deck, which offers views of the mountains to the south. The extension below it on the first floor defines a dining room sheathed in copper. As in the Melville church, the daylight filtering into the gathering area from above helps fill the space with natural light.

The architects designed the living room so that it appears to grow naturally out of the ground. The floor surrounding the living room consists of local, rough hewn stones called "goshan stone" which are used for all the stone details of the house.

The house fulfills the aspirations of the client as a place to contemplate the cycles of nature, as "a retreat in nature allows the silence of the forest to enter into the domestic realm."

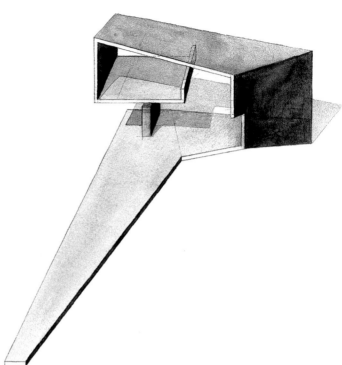

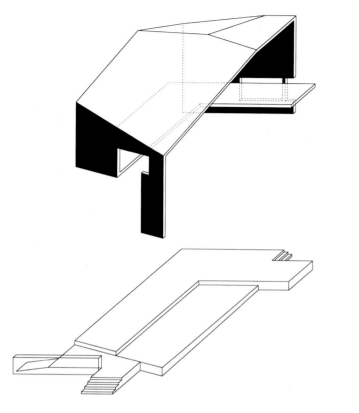

CONCEPT SKETCH

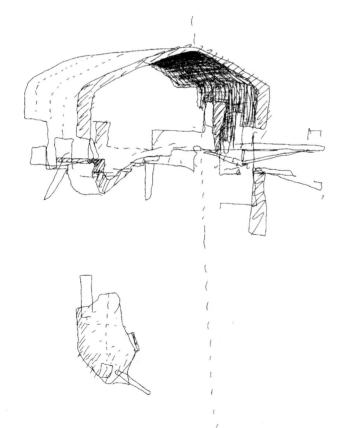

LEFT AND OPPOSITE PAGE: Drawings and floor plans show that the elongated volume stretches on the site, yet has few internal partitions.

UPPER FLOOR PLAN

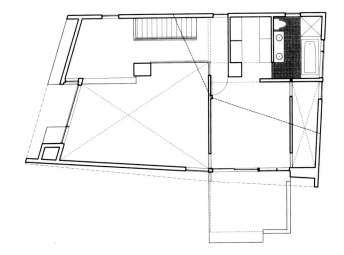

GROUND FLOOR PLAN

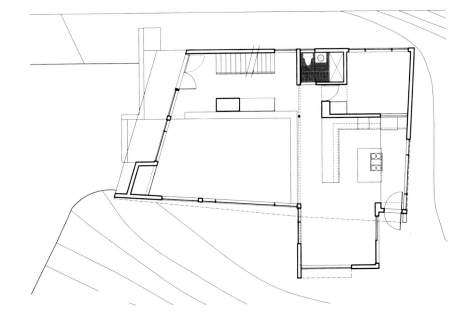

EAST ELEVATION   SECTION

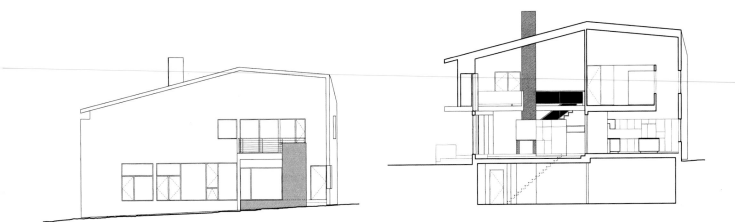

ABOVE LEFT: *The outer shell of the house is constructed of shiplapped cedar.*
ABOVE RIGHT: *The dining room extension is sheathed in copper.*
LEFT: *View of the main entrance elevation.*

ABOVE AND LEFT: *Views of the living area from the dining pavilion looking south.*

RIGHT: *The open-plan interior is filled with natural daylight. The second floor platform, which contains the master bedroom, overlooks the first floor living space.*

LEFT AND ABOVE: *A stainless steel staircase leads up to the second floor loft.*
RIGHT: *View from the second floor master bedroom loft.*

78 Alves Residence

JOHNSON/JONES RESIDENCE

Tucson, Arizona
Jones Studio, Inc.

Photography: Timothy Hursley

RIGHT: Extensive overhangs and careful solar orientation assure complete natural daylight with responsible sun control.

An awkward suburban site had significant bearing on the design of the Johnson/Jones residence. The property is located in the sprawling development of Ahwatukee, near Tucson, next to the public trail head to the South Mountain Preserve hiking paths, but also adjacent to an unsightly water chlorinating tank. The architect used rammed-earth construction to build what has become known as "The Dirt House," a sustainable building that integrates the natural and man-made elements of the site.

The design consists of two simple rammed-earth walls topped by a dynamic flying roof and book ended with cylindrical-block exterior rooms, incorporating the water tank as one end. The intent was to offer hikers several views of the house as they proceed on their trek. The rotated block site walls and metal screen fences create transparent divisions between the public and private land, yet trail users are not "walled out."

Rammed-earth construction provides a highly energy efficient interior. Heat conducts through compacted dirt at a rate of one inch per hour. Therefore, the interior surface remains a constant room temperature throughout the year. Other construction materials have significant recycled content or are resource-efficient materials, such as plywood glued together with toxin-free adhesives, low- to-no-VOC paints; high-performance glazing, engineered-composite framing lumber; rusted steel wall cladding; and concrete block manufactured with fly ash.

Extensive overhangs, a rusted steel louver, and careful solar orientation assure complete natural daylighting with responsible sun control. An eighty-percent-dense "green house" fabric protects the skylight during summer months and is removed every fall.

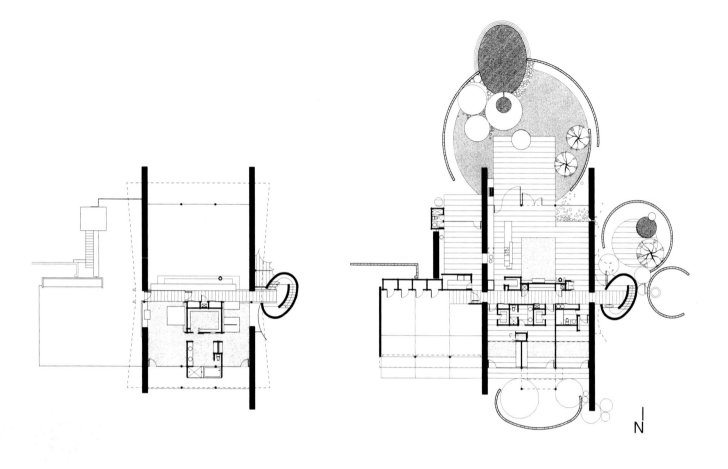

82 Johnson/Jones Residence

RIGHT: *The steel sunshade blocks the warm summer sun, yet lets the winter sun penetrate into the interior.*
LEFT: *The roof is pitched toward the large scupper projecting from the stair tower. Rainwater clings to "rain chains" and is deflected into an eighteen-foot diameter holding area where it overflows into the indigenous, drought tolerant landscaping.*

ABOVE: *View out of the living room*
towards the lily pond.
LEFT: *The main living space receives*
an abundance of natural light.

ABOVE: View from the stair tower.
LEFT: In the main hallway, the sec-
ond floor is clear glass to allow day-
light to circulate to the ground level.

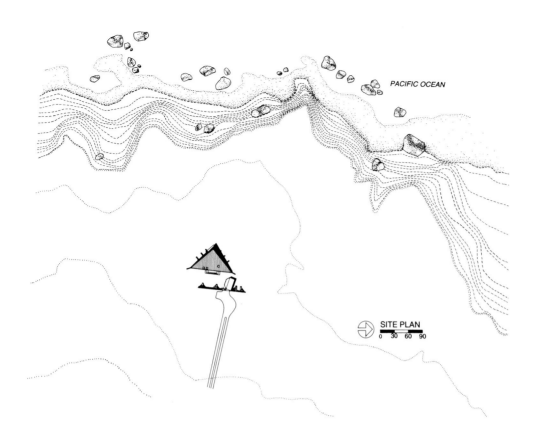

PACIFIC OCEAN

SITE PLAN
0 30 60 90

OREGON COAST HOUSE

Oregon

Obie G. Bowman Architect

Photography: Tom Rider

OPPOSITE: *When approached by land, the prow of the triangular-shaped house points out to sea.*

The Oregon Coast House was designed by Obie Bowman to weather the harsh winds that sweep off the Pacific Ocean at up to one-hundred miles per hour. For the house, Bowman relies on an exoskeleton of Port Orford cedar logs, inspired by the driftwood debris that covers the nearby coastal beaches.

The 1,860-square-foot house is triangular-shaped, with its prow-like nose pointing out to sea. The cedar exoskeleton buttresses the short ends of the triangle, with the hypotenuse containing the trademark Bowman barn doors.

The Oregon Coast House consists of three parts—the house, placed to capture views up and down the coastline; a free-standing garage sited to block prevailing spring and summer winds; and an over-scaled, cedar-log-supported wall that forms a rear courtyard as well as screens the house from its neighbors. To help take in the scenery on calm days, a bleacher-like arrangement of steps leads up to the flat roof of the garage.

The interior is arranged as a series of lateral zones leading from the most public area at the ocean front to the bedrooms at the interior courtyard. Cantilevered out towards the ocean is an elevated loft accessed via a portable, rolling ladder. Excessive heat buildup is controlled by tinted, recessed, low "E" glazing, interior shades, and a passive ventilation chimney located at the apex of the loft.

The final zone contains two bedrooms, baths, and the kitchen. It is fronted by a wall of exposed framing and serves as a library complete with lighting and a rolling ladder. Large sliding wall panels allow the bedrooms to open up to the living spaces to provide spatial relief and additional ocean views. The panels are cement board stained with common garden fertilizers and set in a structural steel frame.

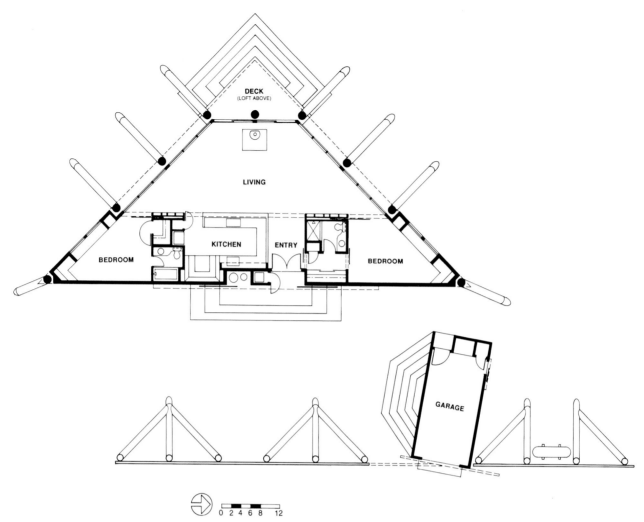

DECK
(LOFT ABOVE)

LIVING

BEDROOM

KITCHEN

ENTRY

BEDROOM

GARAGE

0 2 4 6 8 12

90 Oregon Coast House

ABOVE: An exoskeleton of Port Orford cedar logs buttresses the house.
LEFT: View of cantilevered loft with deck beneath.

91

ABOVE LEFT: North bedroom with sliding door closed.
ABOVE RIGHT: Same view with door open.
RIGHT: The living area looking north.
LEFT, ABOVE: The loft, located in the prow, looks out over the coastline.
LEFT: Dining area looking south.
FOLLOWING PAGES: Pigeon Point aglow at nighttime.

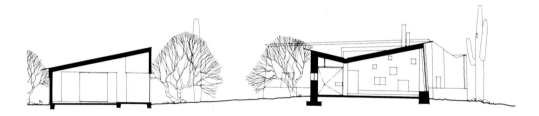

PALMER/ROSE HOUSE

Tucson, Arizona

Rick Joy Architect

Photography: Timothy Hursley

RIGHT: The insulated glass windows of the master bedroom (on the right) and the living room on the north façade reflect the surrounding environment.

In bold geometries, architect Rick Joy combines the tradition of massive rammed earth walls with crisp steel and translucent glass to create a house in profound agreement with its natural environment.

The Palmer/Rose House is located on a four-acre site in the Tucson suburbs several miles from the Santa Catalina Mountain Range. Paramount to the design was preserving the sense of the raw land and the house's connection to it. For design inspiration, Joy looked to the ancient cliff dwellings of Mesa Verde and the undecorated, clean-lined vernacular of the desert and discovered the possibilities of rammed-earth construction. Of the Palmer/Rose house he said, "The basic shell of the building is rough, and within that shell we insert more refined elements as though they are in a ruin."

The program was separated into three segments—the bedroom and living area wings, the combination garage and workshop, and the guest apartment. The bedroom and living areas are similarly shaped structures with butterfly roofs. Each has a main interior room with a large glazed wall offering views and connections to the outside. And each has a rammed earth wall that becomes a focal point of the space. These two segments are connected at a V-shaped entrance that also serves as a privacy shield between the private and public realms. The 1,500-square-foot garage, workshop, and guest apartment section sits across a formal courtyard.

Throughout, sleek steel and glass surfaces are juxtaposed against the rammed-earth walls. Or, in the case of the porch, the rammed-earth wall with fireplace contracts the open-air spaces. There, a pivoting glass door connects the kitchen with the patio.

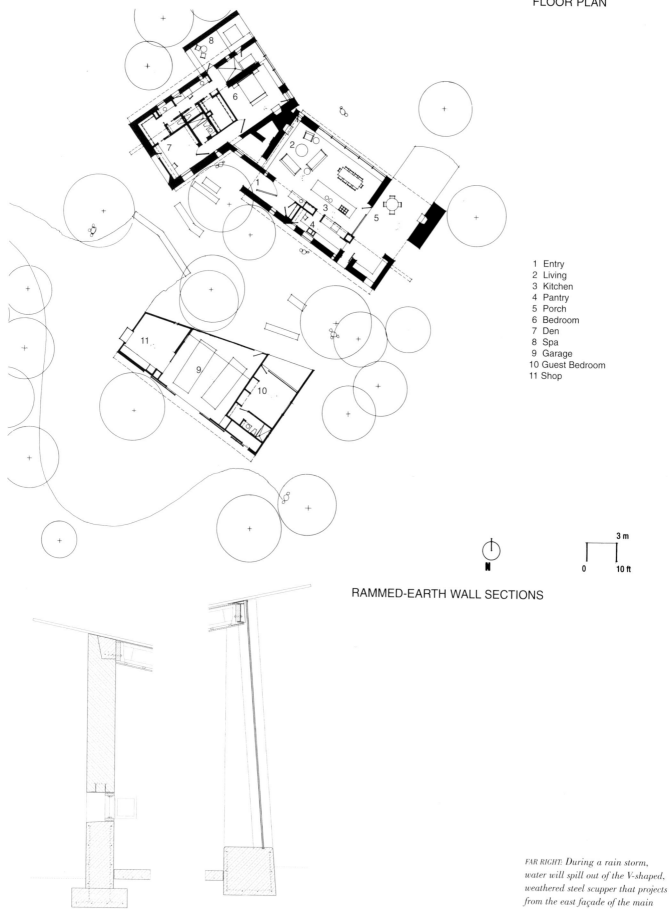

1 Entry
2 Living
3 Kitchen
4 Pantry
5 Porch
6 Bedroom
7 Den
8 Spa
9 Garage
10 Guest Bedroom
11 Shop

3 m

0   10 ft

N

RAMMED-EARTH WALL SECTIONS

FAR RIGHT: During a rain storm, water will spill out of the V-shaped, weathered steel scupper that projects from the east façade of the main house.

ROOF DETAILS

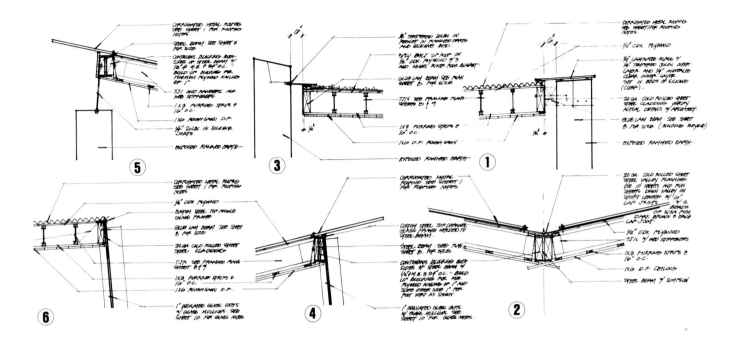

FIREPLACE DETAIL

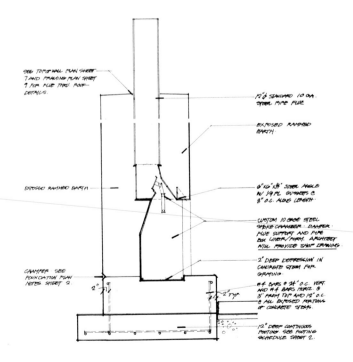

ABOVE: *The outdoor patio extends from the main living space.*
RIGHT: *The patio is flanked on one side by a rammed-earth wall and on the other by sliding glass doors.*
LEFT: *A steel lintel supports the clerestory above the front door.*

ABOVE: *The garage is clad in weathered steel and the house (right) is of rammed-earth construction.*
LEFT: *The rammed-earth sits on a reinforced concrete stem wall.*
RIGHT: *The glass window panes of the master bedroom.*

102 Palmer/Rose House

ABOVE: *Living room with Douglas fir ceiling and rammed-earth wall illuminated by a skylight.*
LEFT: *Kitchen and dining area.*
RIGHT: *Kitchen and dining area with a view to the northeast.*

ABOVE AND RIGHT: The master bedroom wing also has a butterfly roof, which brings natural light deep into the space.
FOLLOWING PAGES: The north façade, with the main living space to the left and the butterfly-roofed master bedroom to the right.

106 Palmer/Rose House

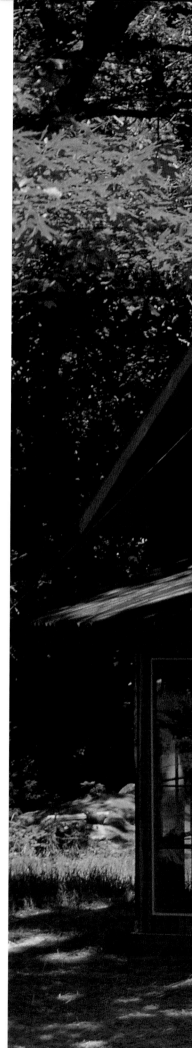

MACKIE HOUSE

Franklin County, Kansas

Dan Rockhill and Associates

Photography: Dan Rockhill

ABOVE AND RIGHT: The house is clad in salvaged corrugated steel and recycled Virginia greenstone.

Dan Rockhill designed this low-cost ($50,000) house for a young couple using only salvaged materials from a local wrecking yard. The concept was to build a flexible space that contained a hierarchy of lofts and alcoves while keeping the building process simple.

The design was actually inspired by the thirty-foot Fink trusses that once supported a Santa Fe Rail warehouse in Kansas City. The architect welded two trusses together to create a glazed truss on the south façade. This form then dictated the overall design—upon the thirty-foot truss Rockhill added another truss, which he rotated 45 degrees. The geometry created alcoves within the open plan into which were inserted bedrooms, a kitchen, and a bathroom, which revolve around a central mechanical core and wood stove. In fact, the building was designed so that it could be constructed in panels on the ground and put together like a model, the parts lifted with a forklift.

Salvaged corrugated metal from a factory and used Virginia greenstone clad the house. A shoji-like screen of the recycled factory window divides the living room for the children's bedroom. The kitchen cabinets were taken from a former high school economics room. Loft railings are former sewer grates, supported by galvanized steel triangles.

Rockhill's fondness for salvaged materials is based on the conviction that the "quality of materials has deteriorated over the last few decades," and that "anything in a salvage yard has endured for decades, and has more decades to go." He has successfully demonstrated that the used goods he finds can be recycled into a thoroughly unique house at a much lower cost than a conventional home.

FLOOR PLAN   AXONOMETRIC VIEW

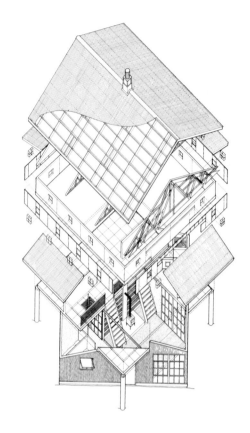

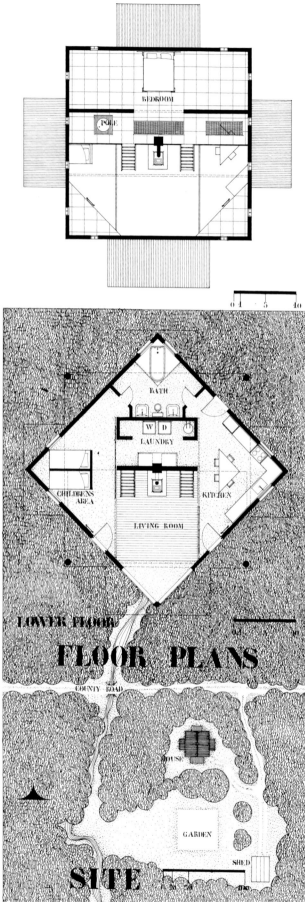

FLOOR PLANS

112 Mackie House

ABOVE: Kitchen.
RIGHT, ABOVE: Living room.
RIGHT: View of the living area and kitchen from the bedroom.
LEFT: The building is a simple form—two thirty-foot by thirty-foot squares, set atop one another, the top one rotated 45 degrees.

ABOVE: A ladder leads to the second floor loft.
RIGHT: The living spaces revolve around a mechanical core and wood stove.

114 Mackie House

DANIELSON COTTAGE

West Pennant, Nova Scotia,
Canada

Brian MacKay-Lyons
Architecture Urban Design

Photography: Brian MacKay-Lyons

ABOVE: *The house sits dramatically*
on the cliffs above Aspy Bay.
RIGHT: *The corrugated steel roof*
inclines up the landward façade,
over the trusses, and descends
halfway down the seaside elevation.

Perched on the cliff's edge on Cape Breton Island, Danielson Cottage has spectacular views across Aspy Bay to Cape North, the North Star, and, on clear days, to Newfoundland. Brian MacKay-Lyons' house frames 360-degree views. The building, and its guest house, is used in a didactic way to explain the landscape.

Designed as a retirement home for a meteorologist and landscape architect on a tight budget, the house takes the form of an archetypal lean-to. It is basically a box in design covered by a corrugated lid dramatically canted upward toward the sea. Built of aluminum and steel, the roof resembles a huge sheet of metal as it inclines up the landward façade, over the trusses, and folds again to descend halfway down the seaside elevation. The canted roof serves as an architectural catch basin, a rain scupper sloped to the south.

Inside, the roof is held in place by wood trusses that span the upper-level bedroom. The top and bottom of the chords align with the ceiling and floor of the second level. On the first floor, the service spaces line the landward façade, freeing up the remaining space for a great room—and magnificent views of the ocean. The fireplace occupies a virtually freestanding concrete-block structure opposite the entry, joined to the house by glass panels that frame views to the north and the south. In the winter, the Danielsons can slide wood panels to cordon off the kitchen, bath, and bedrooms from the unheated living space.

To save costs, much of the house was prefabricated in Halifax. MacKay-Lyons borrowed from the tradition in the Maritimes of "treating buildings like boats—lightweight, mobile structures on land, ice, and water."

FLOOR PLAN

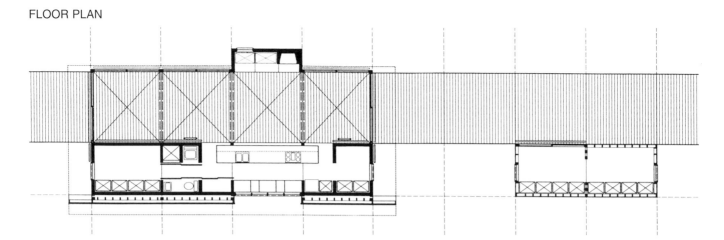

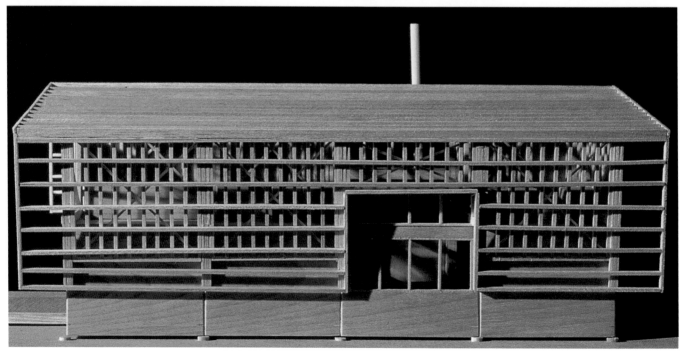

118 Danielson Cottage

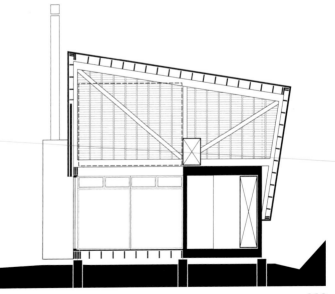

ABOVE AND RIGHT: Stairs lead to the second floor loft.
LEFT, ABOVE: The house has a lantern-like glow at dusk.
LEFT: A model of the house.

120 Danielson Cottage

ABOVE: The metal roof wraps around the house from back to front.
LEFT: Side elevation reveals the trusses on the second level.

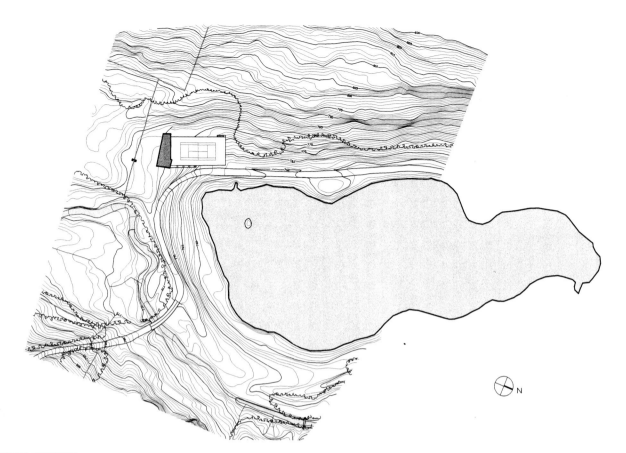

TENNIS HOUSE

Northwestern Connecticut
Gray Organschi Architecture

Photography: Eduard Hueber

Restrictive land-use easements and the natural beauty of meadowland drove the design of this guest house/tennis pavilion. The solution is a landscape-integrated tennis court culminating at a small pavilion that seems to rise out of the land itself.

The architect was taken with the somewhat wild character of the land on this 170-acre estate. Therefore, the design was meant to negotiate between the quality of the site as a former earthwork and its eventual role as a garden and a tennis pavilion.

In the design, the tennis court is cut out of the southwestern edge of the basin that forms the pool. Shaped on three sides by concrete retaining walls, the fourth is defined by removable curtain netting. Clover and vetch will cover the concrete wall to create a natural border.

Because of its location on the Bantam River watershed, the house was limited to a habitable space of less than 600 square feet per floor. Gray Organschi composed a simple wooden box with ten tampered cypress columns. On the main level, a shower room separates the entertainment room from two changing rooms. A second shower is located on the terrace. The lower level, which opens onto the tennis courts, serves as a secondary lounge and bunkroom. An outdoor stair connects the two levels.

The building's trapezoidal shape creates a low corner from which rainwater drains into a concrete basin. Placed between the roof's waterproofing membrane and the soil is a one-and-one-half-inch deep perforated plastic grid formed like an egg carton, which allows for only three inches of soil versus the typical six inches. The roof, punctuated only by a small, concrete chimney and covered with wild grasses, flowering weeds, and sedum, melds with the meadow around it.

RIGHT: The sod roof of the tennis house seems to have been lifted out of the terrain.

AXONOMETRIC

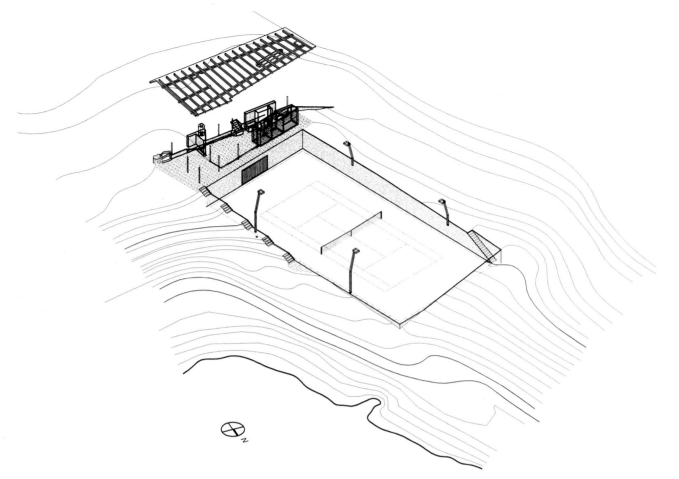

ROOF DETAILS

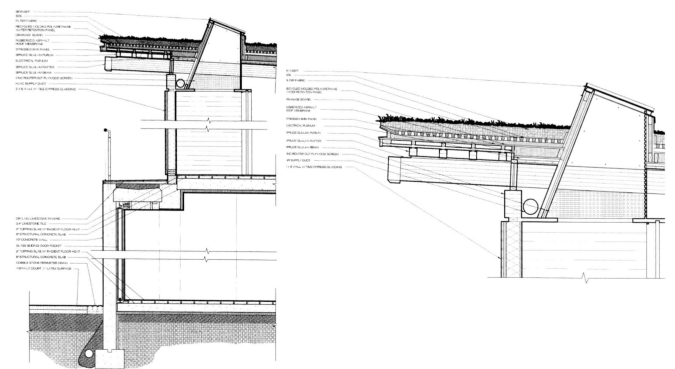

124 Tennis House

125

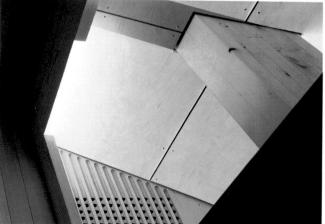

ABOVE: The lower level functions as
an overnight guest house
RIGHT: Bathroom.
LEFT, ABOVE: The courtside patio is
covered by spruce beams.
LEFT: Perforated maple veneer screens
emit daylight deep inside.
FOLLOWING PAGES: The pavilion as
seen from the nearby meadow.

LAKESIDE RESIDENCE

Southwest

Overland Partners

Photography: Paul Bardagjy

ABOVE: *Stairs lead to the main terrace and onto a covered porch and into the main living area.*
RIGHT: *The sandstone wall forms the streetside exterior of the house.*

Approached from the lake, the house rises directly from the water's edge as a series of pavilions linked by deep porches and concrete and sandstone terraces. From inside, each room offers an unique vantage point from which to view the lake.

The house is located on a lot in a densely settled development. It faces the streetscape as a solid stone landscape wall. Yet, behind the wall, Overland Partners created a "surprise house," a complex spatial arrangement of three pavilions connected by porches and terraces, all focused on engaging the lake. Extensive glazing offers panoramic views, while concrete volumes vertically shade terraces from the evening sun. Metal fins shade bedroom windows. Porches protect the liberal glazing while focusing the cool breezes. Glass defines the ostensible limits of the main rooms, but the exterior materials, such as the concrete walls and concrete floors, continue inward bringing in diffuse natural light to blur the boundaries between inside and out.

Arranged around a central garden, the three pavilions consist of the main house—the living, dining, and master bedroom; a four-bedroom block; and the game room and bathhouse activity zone. This configuration easily adapts to the changing numbers occupying the house, ranging from the parents to the entire family of five.

Materials are straightforward, selected for practical and sensual characteristics: monolithic, cool concrete; textural, idiosyncratic sandstone; slick, reflective metal; and warm, smooth cherry wood. The overall image of vertical blocks of concrete emerging from a board-formed concrete plinth was inspired by nearby granite outcroppings.

FLOOR PLAN

1 Master Bedroom
2 Master Bathroom
3 Study
4 Living + Dining Room
5 Kitchen
6 Covered Porch
7 Terrace
8 Stair
9 Bedroom
10 Game Room
11 Garage
12 Boathouse
13 Garden

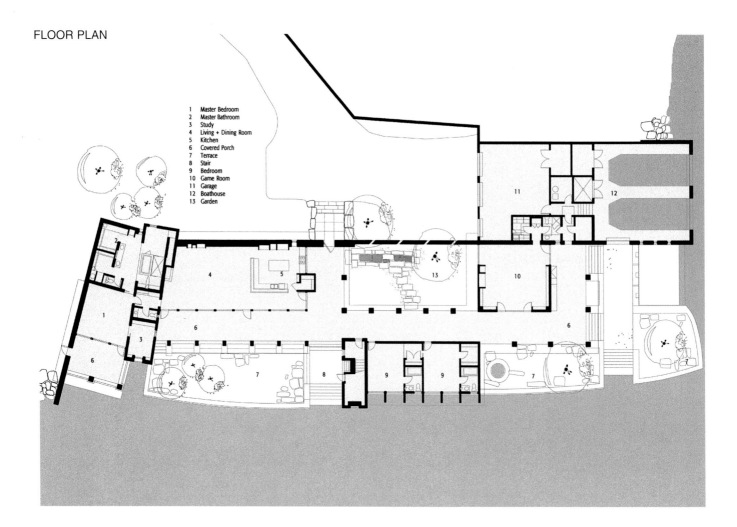

SECTION

132 Lakeside Residence

ABOVE: The garden helps maintain a naturalistic texture juxtaposed against the stone wall and provides a more intimate outdoor gathering area than the lakefront.

ABOVE, LEFT: An intimate seating area in the garden.
ABOVE: The door that leads from the garden into the house.
RIGHT, ABOVE: The covered porch that sits beyond the main living spaces and links the three pavilions.
RIGHT: The terrace outside the game room pavilion.

ABOVE: The pitched roof design created clerestories that allow an abundance of natural light into the living/dining area.

RIGHT: The master bathroom also receives an influx of natural light.

LEFT: Simplicity of form and materials guided the interior design, as seen in the living/dining room.

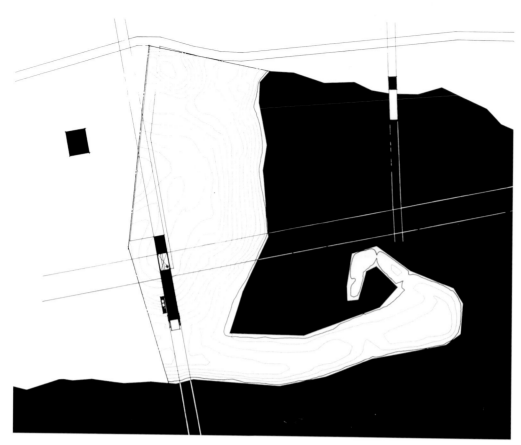

HOWARD HOUSE

Smelt Brook, Nova Scotia,
Canada
Brian MacKay-Lyons
Architecture Urban Design

Photography: James Steeves

RIGHT: The south end of the Howard
House juts out over a breakwater of
rugged granite boulders.

From a distance, the house reads as a corrugated steel-clad wedge emerging from the rugged granite boulders at the waterside. Architect Brian MacKay-Lyons suggests its "rough-and-ready wrapper is in keeping with the rugged cultural landscape context." Its shape acts as a mass that breaks the prevailing westerly winds that shoot across the site.

MacKay-Lyons describes the house as a "monolithic, monopitched shed roof" that climbs to the south and contains one continuous, unobstructed living space. It is a twelve-foot wide, 110-foot-long wall in the landscape.

The cast-concrete foundation rises from the west side, leading up to the entrance. One enters the house through large metal sliding doors on either side. Behind the doors is a skylight courtyard, the centerpiece of which is a large granite boulder. This court acts as a microclimate; when the doors are partially or fully open, there is strong cross ventilation. (Windows on the east side of the house are larger than on the west, controlling summer heat gain, adding to the house's energy efficiency.) A wood-plank walkway leads to a sliding glass door, which opens onto the main living/dining area. This double-height living room has tall steel-braced, aluminum-mullioned windows framing spectacular views of the bay. A cantilevered deck lies beyond. Upstairs, a master bedroom/study overlooks the living room. Three bedrooms occupy the lower level.

Through the use of local materials and forms, MacKay-Lyons has introduced a modern vernacular to the Nova Scotia coast. It is a minimalist design that he hopes illustrates what can be accomplished in an "affordable metal box."

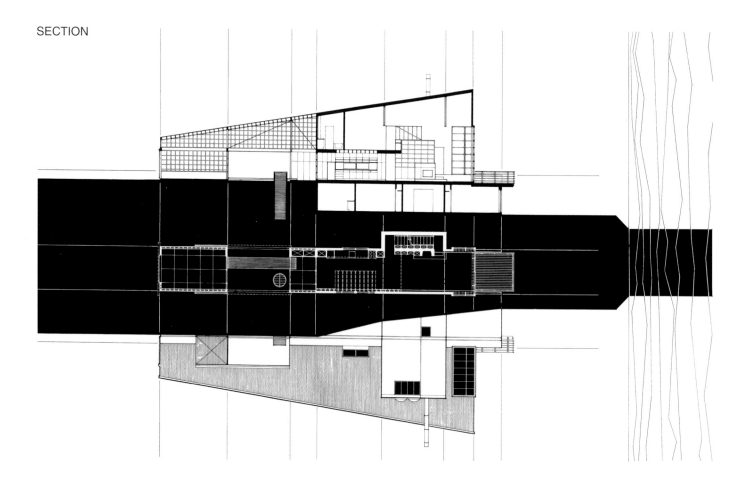

140 Howard House

ABOVE: *The metallic wedge sits upon
a "shoulder pad" of concrete.*
LEFT: *The house under
construction.*

ABOVE AND RIGHT: The tall living room windows—aluminum-framed steel—offer spectacular views of the bay.
FOLLOWING PAGES: A cantilevered deck extends from the main living space.

142 Howard House

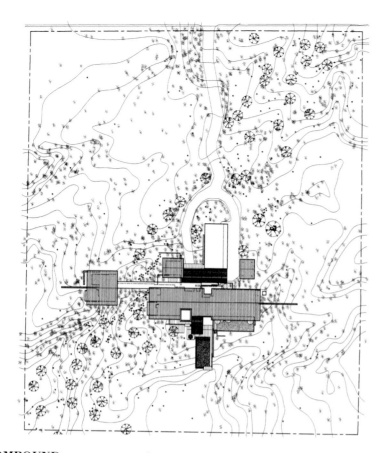

LOW COMPOUND

Scottsdale, Arizona

Jones Studio, Inc.

Jones Studio combined an ancient construction technique with modern environmentally responsible materials to create a desert house with exceptional daylighting, natural ventilation, and energy conservation features.

"What better way is there to integrate a building to its site than to physically utilize the site's excavations for super insulated structural walls?" the architect suggests. The age-old method is rammed-earth construction. To create a rammed wall, scoops of barely-moistened dirt from the site, mixed with five percent Portland cement, are loaded as eight-inch "courses" into heavy wood and steel forms. A hand-held pneumatic tamper–or rammer–compacts the dirt into a rock-hard, sixty-inch, course. This process is repeated until the desired wall height is achieved. The forms are removed, resulting in a very solid, energy-efficient wall system. Standard wall widths are eighteen inches to twenty-four inches. The interior walls are sealed with a clear sealer to keep fine particles adhered together.

Stretching lean and low across the landscape, the 7,800-square-foot house is marked by the subtle sheen of the corrugated metal roof, which is meant to recall traditional ranch houses of the west. On closer inspection, the image shifts to the juxtaposition of the powerful natural rammed-earth walls, the rusted metal siding, and the translucent glass walls that offer desert views inside.

The composition is set on a linear east/west axis with living spaces oriented toward the southern exposure and support functions lining up on the north. Utility runs are consolidated behind a sloped bulkhead that doubles as a natural daylight diffuser for the continuous ridged skylight.

Photography: Timothy Hursley, Mark Boisclair

RIGHT: The compound sits on a ten-acre desert site.

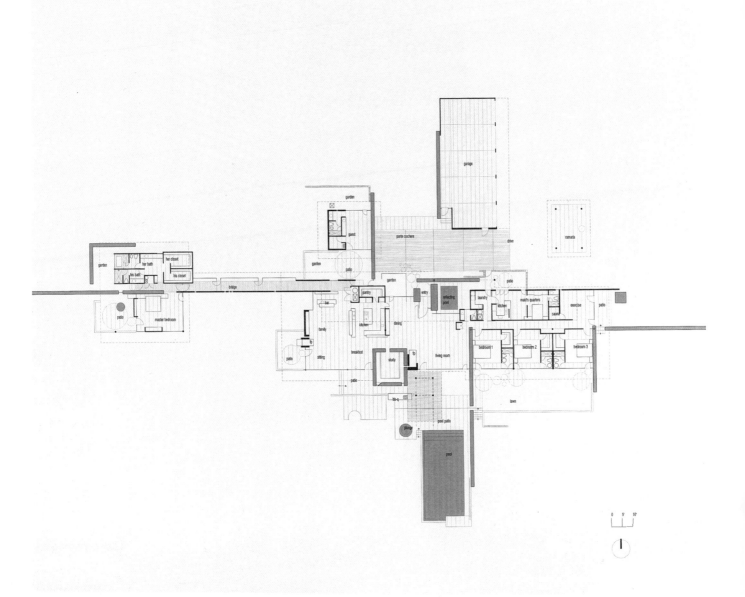

148 Low Compound

LEFT: The house is clad in rusted metal siding, as seen from the entry courtyard.

ABOVE: *From the road, the house purposely appears low and lean.*
RIGHT: *The rear of the house encircles an extensive outdoor patio.*

ABOVE: *The rear patio surrounds a pool.*

LEFT: *The trellis porte cochere at the front entrance.*

RIGHT: *A perfect cube in the main part of the house contains the study.*

150 Low Compound

ABOVE, LEFT, AND RIGHT: *The living/dining area is one continuous space, separated by the kitchen service area. The entire space receives natural daylight from a ridge skylight.*

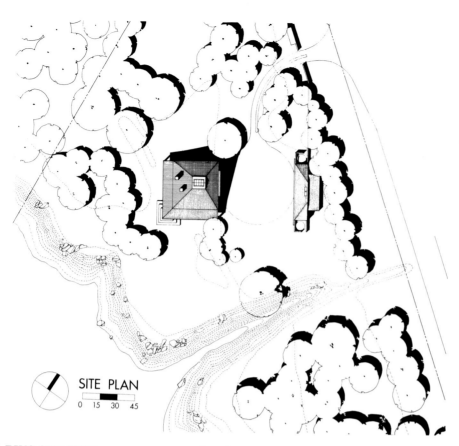

SITE PLAN
0 15 30 45

PINS SUR MER

Point Arena, California

Obie G. Bowman Architect

Pins Sur Mer is sited on a bluff overlooking Schooner Gulch and Bowling Ball Beach in Mendocino County. The design goal was to bring as much daylight as possible into the interior without disrupting the site—a grove of Bishop Pines. This is a naturally foggy and overcast environment, and to make the task even more challenging, the owners requested covered sitting porches on at least two sides.

Obie Bowman's design for the 1,400-square-foot vacation house, therefore, revolves around a high, central skylit entry space that opens to every other room in the house. The entry is demarked by four huge pine columns and becomes the apex of the house and its cultural center, containing an upright piano and a wall of bookshelves, complete with a rolling ladder. Radiating off the central space to the north are the two bedrooms and full baths. The living, dining, and kitchen and spaces are to the south and lead east and west to the two covered porches.

Floors are recycled antique oak and cut limestone, walls are painted gypsum board, ceilings are Douglas fir beams and decking. Cabinets are VGDF. Rumford fireplaces are natural-colored plaster and windows are pine with painted aluminum cladding.

Photography: Tom Rider

The exterior materials are rough 1x12-inch redwood board vertical siding and pointed corrugated metal roofing. A separate garage/workshop/utility structure forms a parking courtyard and acts as a screen between the highway and the house.

Although compact, the design offers a successful combination of private and public gathering spaces, all accessible to what daylight and fresh ventilation is available.

RIGHT: The design goal was to bring as much daylight into the interior as possible while maintaining the natural environment and providing sit-in porches.

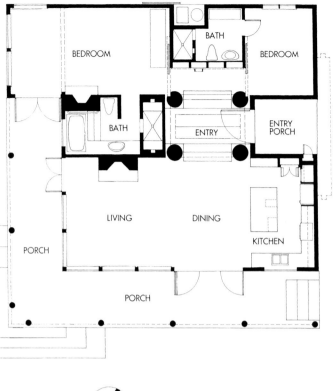

BEDROOM

BATH

BEDROOM

BATH

ENTRY

ENTRY
PORCH

LIVING

DINING

KITCHEN

PORCH

PORCH

FLOOR PLAN

0   5   10   15

156 Pins Sur Mer

RIGHT, ABOVE: Entry with log gutter.
RIGHT, MIDDLE: South façade showing wraparound covered porch.
RIGHT: Porch corners showing columns' relation to surrounding pines
LEFT: West façade.

RIGHT, ABOVE: *Master bedroom look-*
ing towards entry with custom-built
armoire at left.
RIGHT: *Living/dining area as seen*
from kitchen.
LEFT: *Night view through entry to*
library constructed of exposed studs
and blocking.
FOLLOWING PAGES: *South façade at*
dusk.

159

VILLA EILA
Mali, Guinea
Heikkinen-Komonen Architects

Photography: Heikkinen-Komonen
Architects

RIGHT: The north end of the house
reveals the cylinder housing the
guest room.

Heikkinen-Komonen revived the local building method of using stabilized earth in the design of this villa, built for the founder of the Indigo Association, a Finnish nonprofit development organization active in Guinea. The result is a simple house intimately tied to its environment and culture.

The house sits on the western slope on the outskirts of Mali. It is a simple design consisting of a row of independent structures with open spaces in between that act as "porches" looking out to the surrounding scenery. A thatched roof that parallels the slope covers these volumes and voids, making it one long continuous space. The eastern façade, which faces the mountainside, is constructed of woven bamboo. The sun dramatically filters through the bamboo in the morning. On the western side, the yard is terraced with stone walls and planted with fruit trees and bushes.

The architect used the technique of stabilized earth construction (similar to rammed earth) rather than using bricks in the project. Brick burning is prohibited by law in Guinea, as is burn-overclearing of agricultural land, as it drains rivers and adds to the destruction of forests. Manufacturing stabilized soil bricks is an ancient process using a manual brick press. The soil is stabilized with a pinch of cement (three percent to five percent) and pressed in the tiles when the moisture of the mix is exactly twelve percent. Stabilized soil bricks endure pressure very well, but are not very resistant to shear forces and pulling, so the construction work has to be extremely precise. Thermo-dynamic properties are high—the brick stores the night's coolness for the day and the day's warmth for the night. A thin 3mm roof tile was also made on the site with similar tools and only required a little more cement and glass or sisal fiber for reinforcement.

162 Villa Eila

FLOOR PLAN

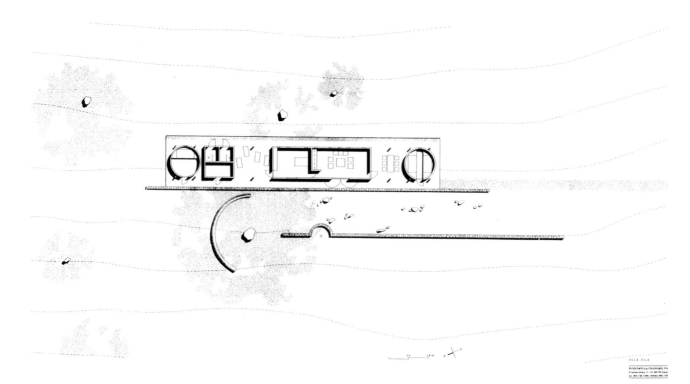

VILLA EILA
Arkkitehtuuritoimisto He
Kristianinkatu 11-13, 00170 Helsi
tel (90) 135 1098, reesfax (90) 135

LEFT: The dining terrace.
RIGHT, ABOVE: View of the front look-ing into the storage room.
RIGHT: At the front, the long hall is flanked on one side by the independ-ent rooms and by the bamboo wall on the other.

164 Villa Eila

ABOVE: Villa Eila sits gently upon the mountain top.

RIGHT: View into the living room and kitchen.

166 Villa Eila

MOUNEY HOUSE

Woodside, California
DeBoer Architects

Photography: Beatriz Cole

ABOVE: The house winds along the edge of the creek.
RIGHT: At the rear of the house is a private outdoor sitting area.

With a restaurant on the front portion of the property, the owner desired a small house that could be a daily respite from her business affairs. Architect Daniel DeBoer saw the opportunity to be highly detail-oriented in his design. He chose to revive the traditional California Arts and Crafts Style, yet used a unique palette of recycled materials.

A creek separates the house from the restaurant. (The creek was restored during the construction project.) A bridge over the creek leads to the front door, which sits at the center of the house. This living/dining space is flanked on each side by the master bedroom suite and the kitchen/guest room wings, respectively as the house stretches along the edge of the creek.

For DeBoer, the measure of a good building is that the occupant and visitors "remain interested in it over time." Therefore, interior textures and colors play an important role, as does the movement of natural light through the building. At the same time, DeBoer is an architect "who collects things," such as materials left over from other construction sites or lumberyards, for reuse. The Mouney House incorporates such materials. The flooring is the lowest grade of white oak, pieces rejected from other construction jobs. The dining room table has Giant Sequoia limbs as its legs and as its top, walnut provided by a residential tree trimmer, and oak salvaged from another construction job. The dining room table bench is made from motorcycle packing crates and the chairs of laminated scraps from a jewelry box maker. Other salvaged materials include wine fermentation tanks and veneered tile counters. The forty-seven windows admit an abundance of natural light into the interiors to highlight these unusual materials.

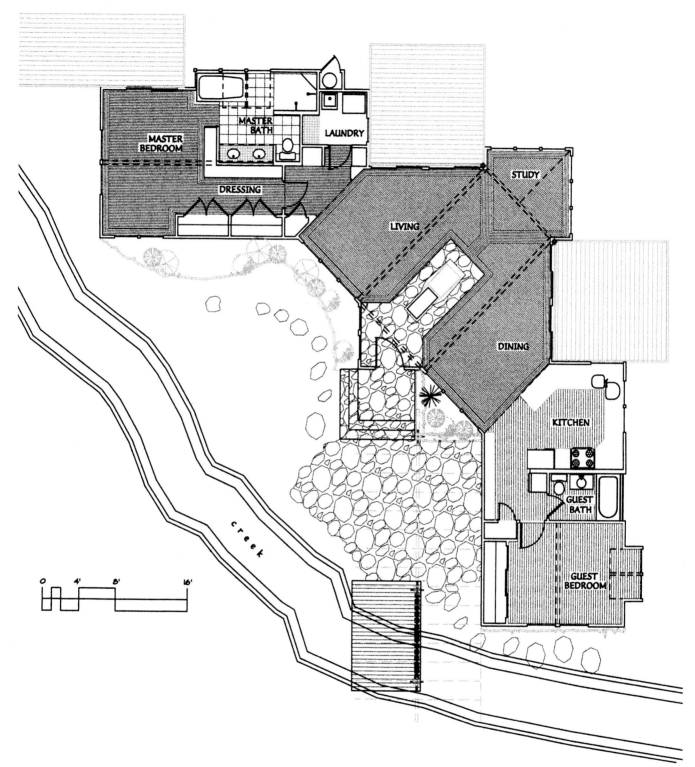

MASTER
BEDROOM

MASTER
BATH

LAUNDRY

DRESSING

STUDY

LIVING

DINING

KITCHEN

GUEST
BATH

GUEST
BEDROOM

creek

0   4'   8'   16'

RIGHT: The kitchen cabinets are edge-banded plywood and the counter is made of marble tile.

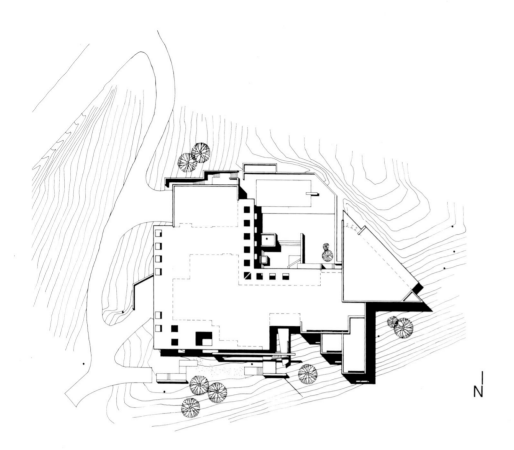

HANSEN RESIDENCE

Tucson, Arizona
Line and Space

Photography: Henry Tom,
Colby Campbell

This 6,000-square-foot desert house for a family of four is designed to take advantage of indoor-outdoor living. Set before the high point of a ridge on a five-acre site in the foothills of the Santa Catalina Mountains, the house is positioned to allow a sense of growth from the site while mitigating the impact on views from neighboring houses. The design, coupled with careful construction, allowed for the conservation of existing vegetation including palo verde trees, giant saguaro, and dense, yellow flowering brittle bush.

Upon entering the house, the visitor catches a glimpse of the mountain view and loses it, only to have it reappear dramatically, framed by a large cantilevered concrete beam structure. This framework serves as the main room, off of which radiate the private spaces. Large areas of covered outdoor space provide pleasant gathering areas. Overhangs and covered patios help maintain the comfort level of the house by shading the expansive glass windows in the summer and providing a gentle transition between the bright exterior and the darker interior space.

As conservation was extremely important, the architect designed two evaporative cooled, tempered exterior microclimates that extend the usability of outdoor spaces and eliminate the need for refrigerating additional interior space. Exterior materials are primarily natural gray split face concrete block, hand-split granite gathered from the site, concrete, and copper. Water runoff from the roof is harvested and stored in a large cistern, and gray water from tubs, showers, and lavatories is reused for irrigation on the site.

RIGHT: A large cantilevered concrete beam marks the entrance to the house.

FLOOR PLAN

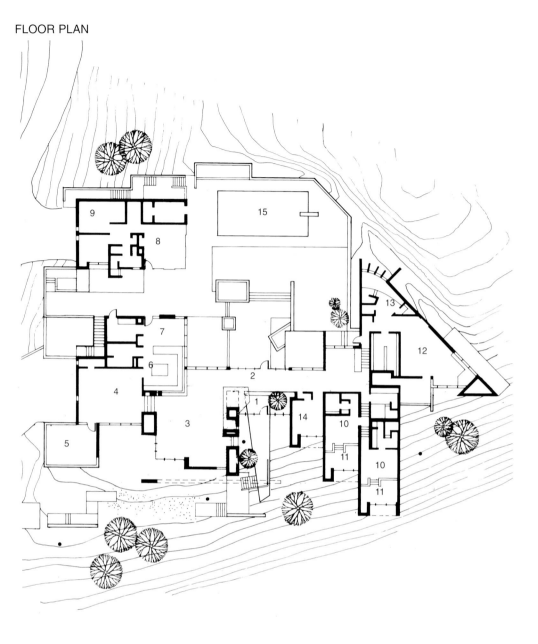

1 ENTRY
2 GALLERY
3 LIVING ROOM
4 DINING ROOM/BAR
5 OUTDOOR DINING TERRACE
6 KITCHEN
7 BREAKFAST ROOM
8 RECREATION ROOM
9 GUEST QUARTERS
10 BEDROOM
11 READING ROOM
12 MASTER BEDROOM
13 MASTER BATHROOM
14 GUEST BEDROOM
15 POOL AREA

SECTION

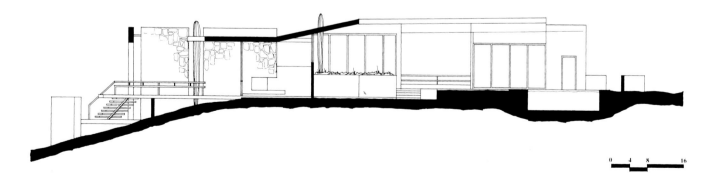

0 4 8 16

176 Hansen Residence

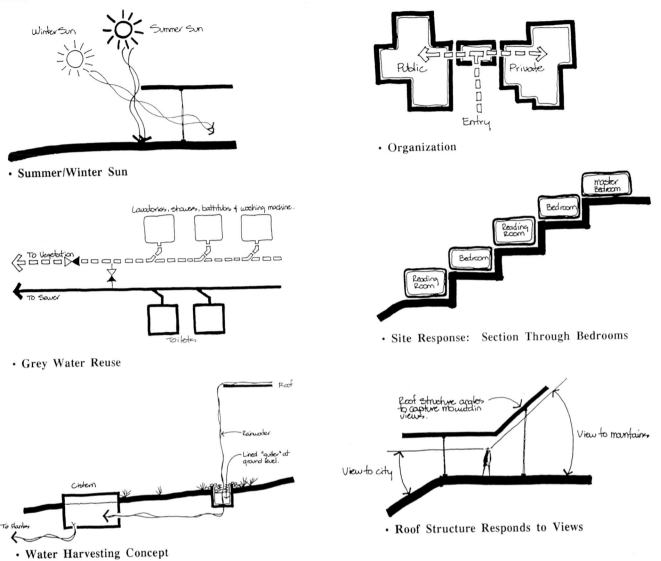

Winter Sun   Summer Sun

· **Summer/Winter Sun**

Public   Entry   Private

· **Organization**

Lavatories, showers, bathtubs & washing machine.

To Vegetation

To Sewer

Toilets

· **Grey Water Reuse**

Reading Room   Bedroom   Reading Room   Bedroom   Master Bedroom

· **Site Response: Section Through Bedrooms**

Roof

Rainwater

Lined "gutter" at ground level.

Cistern

To Planters

· **Water Harvesting Concept**

Roof structure angles to capture mountain views.

View to city   View to mountains.

· **Roof Structure Responds to Views**

RIGHT: The 6,000-square-foot house sits on a five-acre desert site.

ABOVE: Careful construction favored conservation of the existing natural landscape.
RIGHT: Dramatic mountain views inspired the design.

SOUTH TEXAS RANCH HOUSE

Texas
Lake/Flato Architects

For the South Texas Ranch House, Lake/Flato combines two indigenous Southwestern idioms to create a highly energy-efficient house and a dwelling that is exceptionally comfortable in the hot arid Texas climate.

The design consists of a great room connected to a series of single rooms with patios and breezeways surrounding an open courtyard. The great room is the main living/dining area, a light steel-framed elliptical pavilion anchored to the Nueces riverbank by heavy buttress-like stone piers. The openings between the buttresses are sheathed in horizontal screen bands protected from inclement weather by large, operable glass shutters. The pavilion's cupola helps draw the cool river breezes through the house. Opposite the main room at the end of the house, a long arching room overlooks the open pasture.

Connected to the great room are two L-shaped extensions, single room depths that face another around a patio, with breezeways in between. This configuration provides enhanced ventilation and broad overhangs protect the rooms from the direct sun. To create a contrasting experience to the expansive great room, here the architect combined low-slung, stucco sheds as the bedrooms and a steel "truck arbor" to surround the semi-arid courtyard. Flanked by a stock tank, a breezeway completes the courtyard and cools the summer winds as they pass through the adjacent rooms. Rainwater is captured and recycled through a series of cisterns within the courtyard. The sparse, native planting within the courtyard requires minimal watering.

Photography: Michael Lyon

ABOVE: *The house consists of low-slung stucco sheds and breezeways surrounding a semi-arid courtyard.*
RIGHT: *The main living space is anchored to the banks of the Nueces River by heavy stone buttresses.*

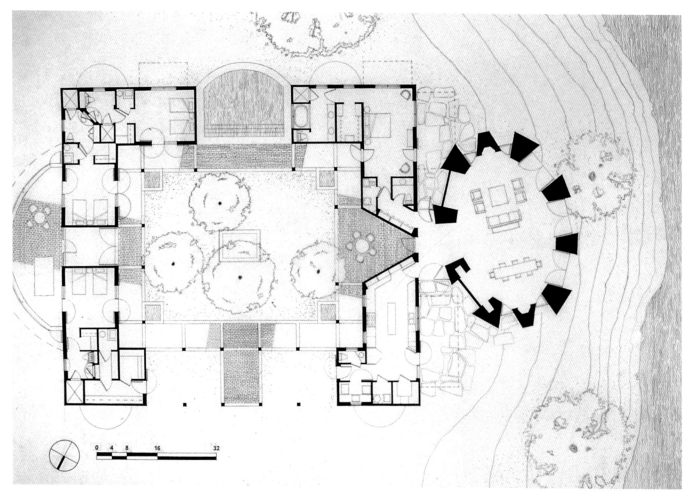

182 South Texas Ranch House

LEFT: View of the courtyard through a breezeway.
RIGHT, ABOVE: The lantern at the top of the great room acts as a ventilator and draws cool air through the house.
RIGHT: Stucco clads the long-slung sheds.
FAR RIGHT: The glazed shutters of the great room only need be closed during the short cold season.

ABOVE: *An intimate bedroom setting.*
LEFT: *The expansive space of the*
great room.
FOLLOWING PAGES: *Cotulla Ranch as*
seen at night.

185

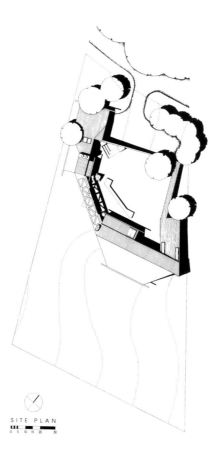

SITE PLAN
0 5 10 15 20 30

TIN ROOF HOUSE

The Sea Ranch, California
Obie G. Bowman Architect

Photography: Obie Bowman

RIGHT: An open truss connects the main and guest houses, the configuration of which forms an inner courtyard.

188 Tin Roof House

The Sea Ranch was first developed in the early '60s on Northern California's coast as a place where nature and human habitation could interact in an intense symbiosis. Obie Bowman's Tin Roof House harkens back to the vigor of the essential idea of "living lightly on the land."

In fact, Sea Ranch gained a reputation as a design haven on the rugged stretch of Pacific coastline ninety miles north of San Francisco. The area is characterized by its unfurled sea, sandstone cliffs, mammal and marine life, and Douglas fir and redwood trees. Bowman has spent much of his career designing houses there and doesn't mind being called a "second-generation" Sea Ranch architect, owing much to the original developers of Sea Ranch, particularly Lawrence Halprin, Joe Esherick, and Charles Moore. Yet, Bowman's is definitely a redefined vision, uniquely his own.

While the Tin Roof House attempts to capture the "lost purity of the California rural tradition," it is also a modern statement. A horizontal composition consisting of two parts, the main house faces south, with an elevated bedroom at the eastern end that overlooks the kitchen and living/dining rooms and the ocean. The guest rooms and baths are stacked in a guest house to the west and connected to the main house by an open-trussed structure. This configuration creates a huge portal on the ocean side and a courtyard away from the ocean, offering privacy, warmth, and protection from the wind. The materials and form merge the silhouette of the coastal barn with the mining shed. Native redwood siding appears as wide-rough sawed "green" boards. Corrugated sheet metal roofing has been left to weather naturally. The main interior space is composed above a continuous wall of niches formed by manipulating and exposing 2 x 10 studs and horizontal blocking.

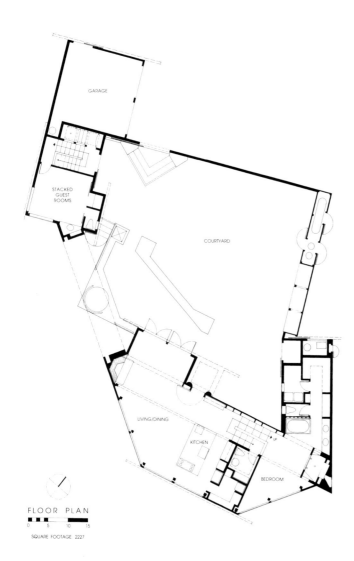

FLOOR PLAN

0 5 10 15

SQUARE FOOTAGE 2227

GARAGE

STACKED
GUEST
ROOMS

COURTYARD

LIVING/DINING

KITCHEN

BEDROOM

UP

190 Tin Roof House

ABOVE: *The rugged nature of Sea Ranch is revealed.*
LEFT: *Entrance to the main house from the courtyard.*

ABOVE: *The dining space in the main house.*
LEFT: *The master bedroom is elevated to overlook the rest of the main house's interior.*

ABOVE: One wall of the main house's living area includes Bowman's signature built-in bookshelves.
RIGHT: Bathroom detail.
OPPOSITE: The broad hearth is sheathed in metallic panels and crowned with galvanized steel flumes.

192 Tin Roof House

McDEVITT HOUSE
Dewees Island, South Carolina

Studio A Architecture
Whitney Powers Architect

Photography: David Edwards and
Studio A Architecture

This property and the one following are located on remote Dewees Island, a 1200-acre barrier island off the coast of South Carolina. It is a vulnerable spit of an island with much of it in wetlands. Accessible only by boat and free of cars, this enclave consists of 150 properties governed by a stringent "green" code. Houses are limited in size to a maximum 5,000 square feet and no more than 7, 500 square feet of disturbed area, including driveways, leaving 95 percent of the island untouched. Existing trees and vegetation must be preserved with minimal impact, and no lawns are allowed.

The McDevitt house is conceived as a minimal outpost with no phones and no television. Well below the maximum building size, it is a mere 1400 square feet surrounded by more than 1600 square feet of screened porches and decks. The house sits lightly upon the landscape on wood piles that soar to the roof level, echoing the trunks of surrounding palmettos and live oaks. A broad metal hipped roof and wide, encircling screened porches provide a refuge from the elements.

Suspended within this shelter are two stacked levels—sleeping and bathing areas within the shelter of the trees. The kitchen and living room are on the top level, above the treetops. The exterior walls are a curtain-like series of glass doors that can be opened up to allow sea breezes and prevailing winds to cool the house.

The design and construction of this house carefully followed the island's covenants encouraging the use of sustainable building materials and technologies. The architect used building materials that included cementious siding, a metal roof, and cotton fiber insulation. The house is also fitted with low water use appliances and fixtures, high-efficiency heat pumps, and recycled content finishes.

ABOVE: The public areas of the house peek above the treetops.
RIGHT: The porches occupy more space than the interior of the house.

FIRST FLOOR PLAN

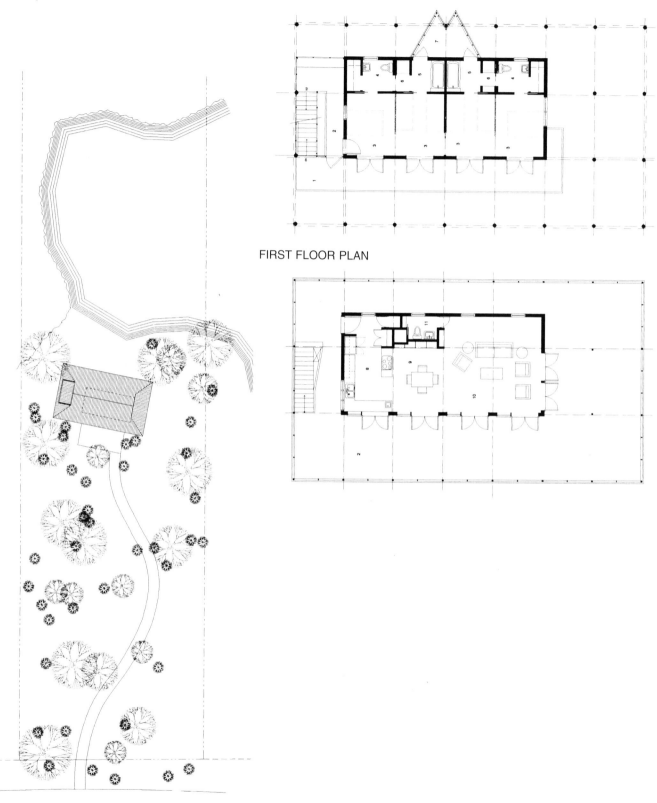

RIGHT: Model views.
FOLLOWING PAGES: Building covenants require that existing trees and vegetation be carefully preserved; porches and decks occupy more square footage than interior space.

196 McDevitt House

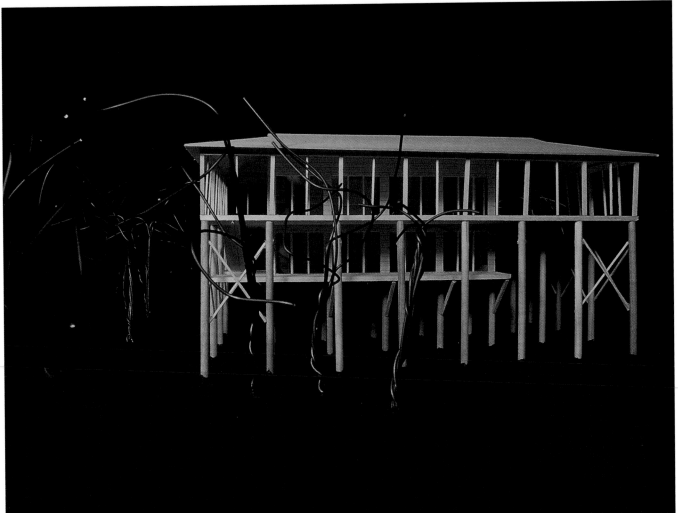

LEFT: *Balconies on north façade.*
ABOVE: *View of porch looking east.*

YOST HOUSE

Dewees Island, South Carolina
Studio A Architecture
Whitney Powers Architect

Photography: Edwin Gardner

This beachfront property, also on Dewees Island, is in a virtually impenetrable jungle of live oaks, cedars, palmettos, and barrier island shrubs and vines. Wetlands bisect and partially surround the property, separating the building site from a line of dunes with a beautiful panoramic view of the ocean.

The basic exterior form of the 3200-square-foot house is that of two simple vernacular farmhouses shifted along the axis to the beach, separated by a gap that mirrors a naturally occurring breach in the site's existing dune line. Bedrooms are located on the first floor with the second floor consisting of public living spaces with prominent views of the surrounding landscape. There is a forty-foot bridge leading from the house to a small seaside pavilion.

Sustainable building practices include floors that are finished with a penetrating sealer, allowing the natural wear of the wood floor to require only occasional spot refinishing. Handcrafted, insulated double-hung cedar windows operate in the traditional top-down/bottom-up arrangement, which along with the numerous French doors, louvered doors in all the bedrooms, and ceiling fans permit a constant ocean breeze to flow throughout the house. A ground-source heat pump is provided for heating and cooling although the air conditioner has yet to be used by the owners, even on 90°+ humid July days. Other sustainable technologies incorporated in the house include the use of low-VOC paints, natural finishes, standing seam metal roofing, and high-efficiency appliances and fixtures.

ABOVE AND RIGHT: The forty-foot bridge connects the house to a seaside pavilion.

SECOND FLOOR PLAN

SITE PLAN

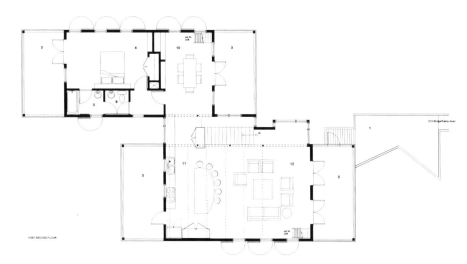

FIRST FLOOR PLAN

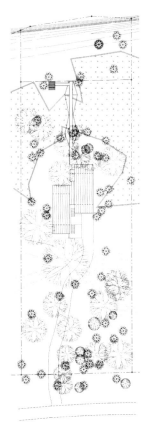

ABOVE: *Model of house.*
RIGHT, ABOVE: *View from ground of bridge.*
RIGHT: *Entry façade.*

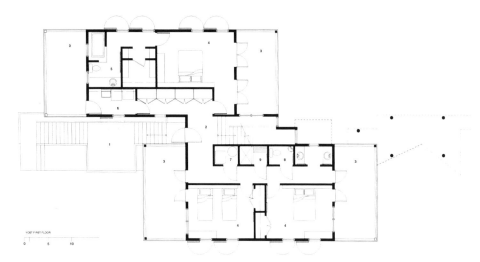

ABOVE AND RIGHT: The bridge is designed to have minimal impact on the existing landscape.

206 Yost House

ABOVE: *View of kitchen from living area.*

RIGHT: *The living area with ladder to the observation deck.*

FOLLOWING PAGE: *View of bridge from dining area.*